DO NOT REMOVE
CARDS FROM POCKET

10 - 16- 89

SUPER BANKING:
INNOVATIVE MANAGEMENT
STRATEGIES (THAT WORK)

SUPER BANKING:
INNOVATIVE MANAGEMENT
STRATEGIES (THAT WORK)

RICHARD B. MILLER

Dow Jones-Irwin

Homewood, Illinois 60430

Sponsoring editor: Jim Childs
Project editor: Jane Lightell
Production manager: Stephen K. Emry
Jacket designer: Sam Concialdi
Compositor: Publication Services, Inc.
Typeface: 11/13 Century Schoolbook
Printer: R. R. Donnelley & Sons

Library of Congress Cataloging-in-Publication Data

Miller, Richard Bradford, 1927–
    Super banking: innovative management strategies (that work) /
Richard B. Miller.
        p.   cm.
    Includes index.
    ISBN 1-556-23114-8
    1. Bank management—United States—Case studies.   I. Title.
HG1615.M56 1989
332.1'068—dc19   88–27564
                                                          CIP

Printed in the United States of America

1 2 3 4 5 6 7 8 9 0   DO   5 4 3 2 1 0 9 8

To Ruth
Who is also super.

PREFACE

Sometimes the headlines in the business press give the impression that the banks of America are being run by dunderheads, charlatans, Las Vegas gamblers, or worse.

Admittedly, much of the news about banking institutions over the past few years has not been good. Mistakes—and we mean really *big* mistakes—have been made. There have been instances of gross misuse of depositors' money. Inordinate risks have been taken, with disatrous results of the first magnitude.

Not only have bankers been hurt by some of these events, but so have employees and stockholders and depositors. And in some instances, the public in general has suffered. The Penn Square debacle, and the ensuing troubles that engulfed (and nearly submerged) such institutions as Continental Illinois, Seafirst, and Michigan National deservedly received considerable attention among bankers as well as in the media. The problems that have hit BankAmerica and RepublicBank in Texas and Chase Manhattan and the Mellon Bank and far too many others have been extremely serious.

The record bailout of American Diversified Savings Bank in California and the failures of thrift institutions and commercial banks in recent years attest to the seriousness of the problems facing many financial institutions in 1988 and 1989.

This negative view of at least a portion of U.S. banking is borne out, to some extent, by the number of banks on the problem list compiled by the Federal Deposit Insurance Corporation. While there has been a drop from the peak of more than 1,600 problem banks in mid-1987 to 1,491 as of March 31, 1988, the figure is still alarmingly high. However, it should also be noted that a majority of the problem banks are located in certain parts of the country—the Midwest, West, and particularly in the Southwest—reflecting the troubles in agriculture and the energy business.

But on the Other Hand

As bad as these statistics are, they also indicate that a substantial number of the commercial banks in this country—some 13,000 of them—are *not* on the problem bank list.

Not only that, bank profits would have set record highs in the first quarter of 1988 if it were not for the (also a record) $1.49 billion loss reported by First RepublicBank Corporation banks. In fact, most banks—87.16 percent, to be precise—were profitable as of March 31, 1988, the best the industry has done since 1983.

Barring the unforseen, 1988, as of midyear, is shaping up as a very good year for a great many banks, and for the industry in general.

In other words, there are plenty of good banks in the United States, and they as doing a lot of good things. Some of the banks are even better than good.

The objective of this book is to accentuate the positive. We take a look at several banks that are doing exceptionally well—and doing absolutely superbly in certain specific areas.

It has not been possible to report on all the excellent banks, so we have zeroed in on a few of the best. Also, it would have been difficult to cover all the different aspects of the banking business, so we have focused on four areas that have particular significance in today's competitive financial environment.

The banks selected and their records of performance also provide some examples that other banks may be able to utilize in their institutions. Lessons and ideas as well as recommendations are spelled out at the end of each chapter.

Every bank included here was visited and key people were interviewed for the purposes of this book. This has been no secondhand effort; it is important to see for ourselves what these banks and these managers have been doing and how they are doing it.

The cooperation and assistance provided this author by all

of the financial institutions and their officers, and their willingness to share their stories with the banking industry, is greatly appreciated.

The examples of banking at its very best may not present applications of use to every banker who reads this book. Still, they do illustrate what can be done—what is being done—in banking today.

ACKNOWLEDGMENTS

To all the banks and bankers who have provided information, time, and cooperation in the preparation of this book, my thanks and appreciation.

I also wish to mention the invaluable assistance I received from several people not specifically mentioned in discussions of their banks, but who arranged meetings and provided much needed information—Russ Hoadley (Barnett Banks), Willis Johnson (SunTrust), Lona Jupiter (Wells Fargo), Melissa Krantz (Republic), Jim Lestell (Hibernia), Sue Rageas (Northern Trust), and Joe Ward (Signet). Also, my thanks to several people whose suggestions of names of banks and bank executives I followed—Dr. Paul Nadler of Rutgers University, Bob Metzger of the University of Southern California, Len Berry of Texas A & M University, and Jeff Kutler of *American Banker*. Last, but never least, my thanks to my editor on this project, Jim Childs; he kept me moving . . . in the right direction.

You all have helped to make this book an interesting and worthwhile project for me.

TABLE OF CONTENTS

AMERICAN BANKING, EUROPEAN STYLE.   LIABILITY
AND ASSET MANAGEMENT AT REPUBLIC.
FOREIGN DEPOSITS.   GROWTH THROUGH DEPOSITS.
THE FLOW OF FUNDS.   DEPOSITOR PROFILE.
DIFFERENT LENDING, TOO.   A WORD ABOUT THOSE
LDC LOANS.   OTHER PROFIT CENTERS.   DEPOSITS
CAN BUILD PROFITS.

HARNESSING TECHNOLOGY.   CONTENDING WITH
COMPETITION.   SOPHISTICATED, SAVVY
CUSTOMERS.   EXPAND OR DIE.   THE HUMAN
FACTOR.   MORE SUPER BANKS.

PART 1

THE MANAGEMENT IMPERATIVE

The key to the success or failure (or points in between) in the world of banking is the caliber of a banking company's management and how well it handles different situations.

This one factor permeates everything a bank does—the services it performs, the controls that have been devised and are exercised, the applications of technology, reactions to adversity, the utilization of human resources, the contributions to the bottom line, everything.

Sure, a financial institution can grow and perhaps prosper with so-so management, although that might be impossible to accomplish if the management is inept. Much depends upon the franchise, the economic conditions, the effectiveness of the competition. But then the question becomes: What might that institution be able to do if better management were in place?

How many times have you considered the situation at a company which has been a client of your bank for a period of time so that you know the firm rather well and said, "It is making money in spite of itself." You may have even thought that about a bank with which you've been associated. Management, in other words, is the prime factor in the life—and death—of a banking company.

However, there are certain activities and certain situations in which management is such an overriding factor that it must

1

be singled out for special attention.   That is why this book begins with the management factor.

   We have selected three such situations, one having two aspects. Each of them has special significance in today's banking climate. There are, of course, other areas that could have been included. But the following are, we think, representative of just how good, and how effective, bank management can be.

CHAPTER 1

TURNING A BANK AROUND
How a Troubled Bank, Michigan National Corporation, Was Returned to Good Health.

We've got trouble,
right here in River City.
—*Professor Harold Hill in "The Music Man"*

It was July 19, 1985. The board of directors of the Michigan National Corporation was scheduled to meet at 2:00 P.M. The major business on the schedule was the election of Robert J. Mylod to be chairman, president, and chief executive officer of the company.

That morning, Mr. Mylod was at the headquarters of the bank holding company in Bloomfield Hills, just outside Detroit, meeting with Semon (Bunkie) Knudsen, the former auto company executive, a member of the board and chairman of the search committee. Knudsen was filling in the soon-to-be chief of the bank with the day's schedule when they were interrupted and given an urgent hand-delivered letter. Mr. Knudsen read it and passed it to Mr. Mylod.

The letter was official notification that Comerica Corporation, a rival Michigan banking company, was prepared to offer $26.50 per share for MNC stock. This was about $9.00 above the current price of the stock, but still only 90 percent of book value. Obviously, the letter added to the urgency of the board's meeting later in the day.

A BANK WITH BIG TROUBLES

The early 1980s had not been very good years for Michigan National. Once it had been the largest banking company in the state, with a reputation as an innovative financial institution. During the late 1970s, however, earnings began to drop off and loan losses mounted. Growth slowed and it fell to fourth place. In addition, the Securities and Exchange Commission investigated the holding company for possible violations of federal securities regulations.

On top of this, the bank started to participate in energy loans written by Penn Square Bank in Oklahoma in an effort to improve its profit picture, following the lead of Chicago's then high-flying Continental Illinois Bank. By the time the Penn Square scandal erupted in the newspapers in 1982, Michigan National had bought about $190 million in loans from that bank. As a result of this unhappy episode, the bank lost about a third of its capital.

That year, MNC earnings were only $4 million (see Table 1–1). The following year was a real disaster, with the bank losing over $5.5 million.

That wasn't all. The chairman of the bank at the time, Stanford S. Stoddard, son of the founder and former chairman of

TABLE 1–1

Progress at Michigan National

	1981	1982	1983	1984
Deposits (in thousands)	$ 5,109	$ 5,544	$ 5,955	$ 5,892
Net Income (in millions)	37,866	4,042	(5,567)	21,437
Earnings per Share	$ 3.34	$ 0.30	$ (0.57)	$ 1.81
Dividend per Share	$ 1.08	$ 1.13	$ 1.20	—
Return on Equity	11.5%	0.7%	(1.5%)	6.4%

	1985	1986	1987
Deposits (in thousands)	$ 6,328	$ 6,759	$ 6,861
Net Income (in millions)	34,427	52,220	73,930
Earnings per Share	$ 2.64	$ 3.48	$ 4.84
Dividend per Share	$ 0.45	$ 1.15	$ 1.45
Return on Equity	8.96%	12.03%	15.09%

the bank, Howard Stoddard, was accused of misapplying bank funds. While both father and son had aggressively built the institution, Stanford proved to be near-dictatorial in the way he ran the bank, sometimes using bank employees to do maintenance work on his homes.

After resigning in the summer of 1984, Stanford Stoddard was convicted of a scheme whereby he owned a building in Jackson, Michigan, and then leased space to a subsidiary of Michigan National at what the U.S. prosecuting attorney called "grossly exorbitant" rates. He was sentenced to three years in jail and barred from banking for life. Mr. Stoddard is currently appealing the sentence.

As might be expected, federal and state banking regulators were concerned about the management of Michigan National, as well as the financial health of the organization.

A GUTSY MOVE

During the fall of 1984, Bob Mylod, who was then president of the Federal National Mortgage Association (Fannie Mae) in Washington, was contacted by a headhunter who had been hired by Michigan National. Was he interested in the job of chief executive of a major regional bank with very serious problems?

He was. Mylod had just about decided that two years in Washington was enough. It was time to get back to the real world. Although he was known primarily as a mortgage banker, he had started his career at Citibank. He had spent a number of years in Michigan (before going to Fannie Mae, Bob Mylod was head of Advance Mortgage Company in Southfield), and his wife and children liked that part of the country.

Not long after visiting MNC officials. Comerica indicated an interest in the bank and that it would probably make an offer. So the letter that arrived on January 19 was not a total surprise, although the timing was, at least, interesting.

When he was offered the post of chairman and president of Michigan National, Mylod told the officials at the bank that he was "not interested in spending any part of my career presiding over the dissolution of the company."

He also told the board he certainly was not interested in selling the company, and that it had enough strength to survive.

After being assured that the bank's board had no intention of selling out, he accepted the job.

To celebrate the move, Mylod had promised his wife a vacation in London, once he had officially joined the bank. Although the formal offer from Comerica served to complicate matters, Mr. and Mrs. Mylod left on their trip right after the board meeting.

Two days later, Comerica attorneys got in touch with Michigan National officials. They complained that a bona fide offer had been made, and if the bank did not make the offer known to its stockholders and to the public, Comerica would have to take legal action.

The Mylods were advised of this latest development and immediately returned to Detroit. Bob Mylod was facing the dual task of fighting a hostile takeover bid and turning the bank around.

FIGHTING OFF THE TAKEOVER ATTEMPT

There have been few hostile takeover attempts in banking, so there are few ground rules to follow. The new chairman and president of Michigan National nevertheless wasted no time in marshalling his forces to turn back the Comerica bid.

His first step was to change investment bankers. He chose a firm with which he was familiar, one that included members he had known for some time and with whom he felt comfortable.

"Comerica tried to get me to talk with them," Mylod said. But he refused to set up a meeting.

"Then, about a month later," he said, "they came back to us and advised that the offer they made was low and that the MNC board had every right to reject the offer."

Somewhat surprisingly, Comerica did not increase its bid. Instead, it did a lot of maneuvering, and went about taking steps to force a proxy fight. Permission was granted by the authorities.

Michigan National and Mr. Mylod were not sitting idly by while all this was happening.

It is so happened that MNC was one of the few banks in the country with a stock bonus plan. It was devised to give the employees the ability to vote their own stock. Up to that point, the stock was held in trust, with a senior management committee acting as trustee. Allowing employees to vote their own stock—a privilege they continue to enjoy today—helped to enlist them in the efforts to turn aside the takeover attempt.

As owners of over 20 percent of the corporation's stock, the employees were and are the largest stockholder group. Their support was essential if the bank were to remain independent.

Many of the staff people at MNC were more than willing to do battle against Comerica. They wore "Nomerica" buttons and officers distributed T-shirts with the same inscription.

That spring, MNC ran an advertising campaign on television, portraying the bank as a family unit fighting an outsider, with Bob Mylod as an "Iacocca-type" spokesman. Viewers were asked for their comments concerning the takeover attempt; most of them were pro-Michigan National.

These visible efforts helped to change the image the employees had of their organization. The efforts also improved the image the public had of the bank.

"Comerica's spotlight shone a positive light on the bank," Mr. Mylod said. Investors began to figure that if another bank wanted it, Michigan National must be worth something. As a result, the stock rose to $31 a share.

Still, the fight was far from over. By summer, according to Bob Mylod, it "was obvious we had to raise capital to offset the Penn Square losses and start to rebuild the bank." Two moves were taken in July, 1985:

• Marine Midland Bank bought a 4.9 percent stake in MNC. This increased primary capital by $20 million.
• An employee stock ownership plan (ESOP) was created, giving employees an additional 10 percent ownership in the company and boosting primary capital by another $38 million.

In addition, the Board instituted a rights offering, a poison pill which would allow the bank two years in which to turn things around. A better term as far as Comerica was concerned, Bob Mylod commented, would be to call it a "sleeping pill."

Then, in August, the U.S. Department of Justice expressed its opinion that a buyout by Comerica would harm competition by concentrating too much of the Michigan markets in one banking company.

Three months later, in November 1985, Comerica gave up on its acquisition attempt and withdrew its offer, ten months after the battle formally began.

TURN AROUND, NOT TAKE OVER

According to Bob Mylod, the seriousness of the situation at Michigan National really hit home when he conducted his first board meeting.

"Twenty-five regulators—they outnumbered our directors—entered the room and proceeded to tell us what the bank had to do to lift the sanctions that had been placed against 11 of our 23 banks," he said. Most of the problems had developed during the tenure of Stanford Stoddard.

While the bank certainly had plenty of problems, Mylod pointed out that when he came on board, MNC had a number of strengths:

- The retail network was the largest in the state.
- The credit card business was the biggest in the country.
- The bank had a strong middle market business.

However, it was still necessary to make the most of those strengths and correct the problems that existed. The strategy Mylod formulated to get MNC back on track had three parts: control, profits, then expansion.

His first concern was control, and he has been accomplishing much of this through the personnel of the bank.

"One of the problems," Mr. Mylod noted, "is that there were too many chiefs." During his three plus years with MNC, there have been two reorganizations. Some people have left because of the changed environment he has brought to the bank. Others have left through attrition.

Still, of the 50 top officers in place when Mylod joined Michigan National, 40 remain, although there have been some reassignments. For example, Lawrence Gladchun, who had been legal counsel, is now a senior vice-president and head of one of the bank's regional offices.

Mr. Mylod has brought in three key officers: K. Larry Hastie, who is executive vice president in charge of investment banking; Eric D. Booth, the executive vice president in charge of administration; and Peter K. Thomsen, executive vice president responsible for commercial, consumer, and mortgage banking. Hastie is a former executive with the Bendix Corporation; Booth was chief financial officer at Advance Mortgage under Mylod; and Thomsen was a senior executive at Citicorp Bank in Chicago.

Because the bank has been able to expand, and the profit picture has brightened considerably, Michigan National has not had to endure any significant reduction in personnel. The bank now has approximately 6,600 employees; this compares with a work force of about 7,000 when Mylod became chief executive.

One thing Mylod insisted upon in early 1985 was to have the support of the board of directors. There have been a few changes to fill the need for new players who would back him up. That support continues today, he said. "Without it, we couldn't have performed as well as we have."

He and his team have also built a comprehensive budgeting process and established a results-oriented planning program. "A lot of planning had to be done," Mylod said, "and the bank is still adjusting."

The entire loan portfolio of the bank has been reexamined and, where necessary, redocumented. This has eliminated major discrepancies and significantly tightened collateral control— two areas that had been the focus of concern by the banking regulators.

In May 1986, the regulators returned to the bank and removed all of the sanctions that had been imposed against the 11 individual banks. One of the regulators later commented that what the bank had accomplished "was the quickest turnaround of any bank with which I've been involved."

You can be sure that Michigan National is maintaining the best possible working relationships with the regulators that it can.

TOO MANY BANKS

One of the major problems confronting Mr. Mylod when he took charge was the fact that the holding company had too many separate bank charters. "We had 23 banks operating in 23 different ways," is the way he put it.

After the banks were sold in 1986, and after the state of Michigan changed its laws to allow consolidations, 15 of the 21 remaining charters were combined in March, 1987.

"Our organization is leaner, more responsive to customer needs, and much more modern in its approach to the current banking environment," Mylod explained.

This restructuring has gone a long way toward accomplishing the first two objectives of Bob Mylod's turnaround strategy—control and profits. The consolidation:

- Streamlined accounting functions.
- Reduced federal reporting requirements.
- Allowed for increased and more efficient customer service.
- Substantially increased the legal lending limit of the bank as a whole.
- Provided access to all banks regardless of geographic location.

THREE YEARS OF ACOMPLISHMENTS

The results of the past three years under Bob Mylod's leadership are evident in the performance figures posted by the bank (see Table 1–1).

During this time, the chief executive of Michigan National has covered considerable ground, in addition to the measures already mentioned.

In the personnel area, Mylod has

- Encouraged an entrepreneurial attitude among employees.
- Tried to get staff people concerned with excellence.
- Instituted performance reviews.

- Established a bonus program based upon performance. (Approximately 25 percent of the people won bonuses in 1987, the first year the plan was operational.)

In operations areas, Mr. Mylod has

- Consolidated the preexisting nine regions into three.
- Centralized asset/liability management.
- Changed computer vendors, with new software installation completed in the summer of 1988.
- Closed 144 branches within a two-year period.
- Implemented a bankwide program that emphasizes customer service.

Shareholders have benefitted rather well by the turnaround. The price of the stock has continued to rise. In addition, increased profits have allowed quarterly dividends to be increased to 45 cents a share, the highest in the bank's history.

All this does not mean there have not been problems.

One of these is third world debt. Fortunately, this was one area where Michigan National was not heavily involved. But early in 1987, the bank reported that its $28 million in LDC loans were to state-owned companies in Mexico and that interest payments were current. The situation changed, and by the end of the year, management decided to charge off half the loans and put the other half on a nonreferral basis.

Potentially more serious were threats to the morale of MNC employees. In December 1987, rumors circulated and reached local news media concerning layoffs and reductions in benefits. Mylod sent a letter to all employees discussing each area mentioned in the news accounts. He told them that cutbacks were contemplated, but that perhaps 75 people would be leaving the bank during 1988, and some of them would leave because they refused reassignments. He refuted a number of other allegations and asked for the support of the staff as the bank continued to meet the challenges of the competition.

As part of Mylod's emphasis on service, employees and customers were asked last year what kinds of things the bank did wrong, as well as what things the bank should be doing that it wasn't doing. Mylod feels that service is the only area in which

Michigan National has not made the turnaround. In other respects, he believes the turnaround actually had been accomplished by the summer of 1987—within the two-year period envisioned by his "sleeping pill" promulgated in 1985.

POISED FOR EXPANSION

The third phase of 49-year-old Robert Mylod's turnaround strategy, expansion, is already being implemented, although the steps taken to date have been measured.

Expansion moves have been made in all three of Michigan National's major business areas—retail and commercial banking, investment banking, and mortgage banking.

More specifically, a charter for Independence One Bank, based in South Dakota, was approved in 1986; today, the bank handles all of MNC credit card receivables. And in 1987, Morison Asset Management Company was acquired and operates as the bank's investment advisory service.

In 1988, MNC announced that it will expand its consumer investment program with PAMCO Securities and Insurance Services throughout its 200-branch system. This follows a pilot program that proved to be extremely successful.

Also, it is reported that the bank is looking at the possibility of buying some banks outside Michigan, most likely in one or two of the five neighboring states in which acquisition is allowed under Michigan's reciprocal banking law.

The progress made by Michigan National during the last three and one-half years has made the bank a far more attractive takeover prospect than it was in early 1985. Bob Mylod, however, tries to squelch that possibility as strongly as he can.

"We're not looking to be acquired and we don't expect to be," he declared. "We expect to be a survivor."

As one financial writer observed, any outsider coming in "would be hard-pressed to top the performance of Mylod's administration."

On the subject of hostile takeovers, Mr. Mylod does not believe they are good for banks, although he doesn't think they are bad generally. However, he believes that takeovers and rumors of takeovers "probably put increasing pressure on banks to improve themselves." That aspect certainly is of value.

He also believes that in order for Michigan National to survive as an independent financial institution and continue to grow, it will need assets of about $30 billion—four times its current asset base. He also feels the bank will need to double its present market capitalization of $625 million. Those are tall orders.

Bob Mylod also predicts that the bank's return on equity will reach 18 percent in 1988, up from 15 percent in 1987. As he puts it, "If you get a good bunch of people together, you have a good chance of success." "Moreover," he adds, "there are a lot of good people here who are working very hard."

His track record to date would indicate that he knows what he is talking about.

A GOOD ROLE MODEL

What Robert Mylod and his people have accomplished—and are continuing to accomplish—at Michigan National provides some solid guides other banks needing realignment and rejuvenation might well consider.

In no special order, here are some that come readily to mind.

• There is an imperative need to institute adequate and effective controls to make sure things do not get off track again. Procedures should be put in place as soon as practical to guard against further slippage.
• Budgets should be devised with dispatch, and then strictly adhered to.
• Personnel should be motivated, not demoralized. While staff reductions may be essential, they can be handled with care and concern for those involved.
• New management people, where needed, should be brought in quickly. In almost every case, some team members should be added who can—and will—work with the new management.

• Information pertaining to what management plans to do should be disseminated quickly. Uncertainty breeds unrest and unrest breeds disarray. And disarray means even more trouble.
• Problem areas should receive priority attention, with solutions put into effect that truly address those problems.
• Management should work with the regulators on procedures that will correct deficiences that may exist.
• A strategic planning program should be instituted without delay; implement those plans with dispatch.

The emphasis here is to move quickly. Depending upon the circumstances, time may be the most difficult factor, even the deciding factor, in turning things around.

A complicating factor in Michigan National's situation, of course, was the hostile takeover attempt that just happened to coincide with the installation of new management. Actually, this was used effectively to get bank employees at all levels involved in the turnaround process. It also was used to build the image of the bank in the eyes of the public. Had this not been the situation, other means would have had to be employed to boost public confidence in the viability of the bank in order to hold on to customers and attract new ones.

One final point: The hostile takeover bid was handled superbly. Other banks faced with a similar situation would do well to study precisely what was done by Michigan National, perhaps even asking for advice on how to apply the measures taken to their own situation.

CHAPTER 2

COPING WITH MERGERS AND ACQUISITIONS

One of the features of banking in the United States in the late 1980s is the prevalence of mergers and acquisitions.

Large banks are acquiring small banks and sometimes vice versa. Banks of all sizes are joining together to form different organizations. Thrifts are joining with other thrifts. Banks are acquiring thrifts. And nonbanking companies are adding banks and thrifts to their organizations. Names are changing and so are the variety of services the merged financial companies are offering in the marketplace.

The variety of mergers and acquisitions is nearly infinite. And, because of the variety of reasons or objectives that are in play that bring financial firms together, there are few combinations that will not gain eventual regulatory approval—assuming the acquirer has the financial depth to sustain the proposed acquisition.

The proliferation of reciprocal banking legislation by individual states also means that federal laws barring interstate banking are effectively being breached. While all this is going on, the talk continues that Congress may pass a new law allowing full interstate banking, but it won't be long before bankers will say, "Who cares? It's here already."

Regardless, the merger and acquisition trend does not appear to be slowing down. The desire to have bigger (and sometimes better) banking companies is seemingly insatiable. Much of this is being driven by efforts to maximize the value of a bank's stock, although things don't always work out the way they had planned.

Of course, there are differences between a true merger and a true acquisition, and that is why an example of each is provided here.

AN INTERSTATE MERGER OF EQUALS

How Sun Banks and the Trust Company of Georgia Got Together—and have Stayed Together

Everything that can be
invented has been invented.
—*Charles H. Duell, Commissioner Patent and
Trademark Office 1899*

ATLANTA/ORLANDO, July 2, 1984: Sun Banks, Inc., a Florida bank holding company headquartered in Orlando, and Trust Company of Georgia, an Atlanta-based bank holding company, today announced they have entered into a definitive agreement to establish a new regional company by combining the two existing companies under a new name, SunTrust Banks, Inc. The boards of directors of both companies have voted unanimous approval of the plan to bring these two banking organizations together on an equal partnership basis.

That announcement was really big news at the time. Perhaps even bigger news is that this first major arrangement under the many reciprocal interstate banking laws proliferating in the United States is working out even better than expected.

The news release issued when the merger was announced explained part of the organizational and financial arrangements.

The combination would be accomplished by forming a new regional interstate bank holding company, of which Trust Company and Sun Banks will become wholly owned subsidiaries. The new regional holding company, SunTrust Banks, Inc., will have its principal holding office in Atlanta and corporate offices in both Atlanta and Orlando. Sun Banks, Inc. will continue to have its own board of directors, as will Trust Company of Georgia. Sun Banks, Inc. headquarters will continue to be in Orlando. Trust Company's headquarters will continue to be in Atlanta.

The banks in the two groups will continue to operate under their present names within their respective states.

The board of directors of the new company will have equal representation from Trust Company and Sun Banks. Robert Strickland, 57, Chairman of the Board of Trust Company, will become Chairman and Chief Executive Officer of the new company. Joel R. Wells, Jr., 55, President and Chief Executive Officer of Sun Banks, will serve as President of the new company.

The agreement provides that approximately an equal number of shares of the new company would be issued to the respective stockholders of Trust Company and Sun Banks. The shares of the Trust Company common stock would be exchanged on the basis of one share of common stock of the new company for each Trust Company share. The shares of Sun Banks common stock would be exchanged on the basis of 1.10 shares of the new company for each Sun Banks share, a ratio based on the lesser number of shares of that company.

When announcing the agreement, Strickland and Wells issued this joint statement:

> We strongly supported passage of the reciprical interstate banking legislation in our states in our mutual belief that the future economic strength and development of this region demands larger banking entities with greater capacity. We are confident that our proposed combination will have far-reaching, long-range benefits for our respective companies, employees, and the markets which we serve.
>
> Our two companies have enjoyed a long and close relationship, and we know each other well. We are both committed to high-quality service and attention to the needs of our customers. We share a similar philosophy about the operation of a strong, sound, and profitable banking business.
>
> The proposed combination is a logical step ahead to insure our leadership position in the rapidly changing and highly competi-

tive environment for the delivery of financial services. This combination has significant, positive implications for the economies of Florida and Georgia. We are enthusiastic about the opportunities this will present us to be of broader service.

AN ADDITIONAL PLAYER

Just over a year following implementation of the agreement to merge, SunTrust Banks announced another agreement in which the Third National Corporation, a Tennessee bank holding company, would join SunTrust.

In a joint statement (quite similar to the statement issued when SunTrust got together), Robert Strickland and Third National Chairman Charles J. Kane said, "The proposed combination of Third National with SunTrust is a logical step forward in the current, rapidly evolving era of regional banking. We have known and respected one another for a long time and our banks have maintained an excellent and productive correspondent banking relationship for many years. Our philosophies for operating a sound, successful financial services business are very similar."

Strickland, in the same statement, added, "Third National has one of the very best track records of earnings of all bank holding companies in the United States. We are very pleased at the prospect of our association with a management and employee group which was so successful. The addition of Third National's strong position in the Tennessee market to the positions enjoyed by Sun Banks in Florida and Trust Company in Georgia will create additional strength and diversification."

Third National continues to be headquartered in Nashville and operates with its present management and board of directors as a wholly owned subsidiary of SunTrust, in keeping with the decentralized practice of Sun Banks and Trust Company. Third National has responsibility for the entire Tennessee operation—including any future in-state mergers or acquisitions it might contemplate. There have been no changes in the names of the corporation or the banks in the Third National group.

Third National has representation on the SunTrust board of directors and executive committee, and its officers participate on the management committee of SunTrust.

SUN TRUST—THE MERGER AND BEYOND

The two men who head up SunTrust are the two who were (and still are) in charge of the two major units of the organization— Trust Company of Georgia and Sun Banks, Inc. Robert Strickland is chairman of the board and chief executive officer; Joel R. Wells, Jr., is president.

The following discussion of the joining together of two regional banking powerhouses into one even more powerful super regional financial institution is based on separate interviews with Mr. Strickland and Mr. Wells at the Atlanta headquarters. When the announcement of the merger was made on July 2, 1984, many in the banking industry were surprised, but the management of the two banking companies felt it was a natural move.

MR. STRICKLAND:

We never talked with anyone else; Florida is the fastest growing area in the country.

MR. WELLS:

We figured it would be good to get together with the Trust Company of Georgia (TCG); together we would be the best in the Southeast. . . . The merged organization makes it possible for us to do a better job at the local level.

MR. STRICKLAND:

The company now operates 52 banks. The responsibility for running them is at the unit level.

MR. WELLS:

Rather than merge the two companies into one or the other, we set up a new company.

MR. STRICKLAND:

The name of "SunTrust" was selected because it is important to have your name known in company board rooms.

MR. WELLS:

In addition, the idea was to keep the names that have enjoyed a good reputation.

Concerning the Location of Corporate Headquarters

MR. WELLS:

There was no discussion about it, and no argument. Atlanta was the obvious choice. After all, Atlanta was the site of the largest bank, and it is the largest market. After all, you have to look at the big picture; it wouldn't have worked in Orlando (Sunbank's main office).

On the Merger of the Two Organizations

MR. STRICKLAND:

In getting together, we had a year to work things out before the merger became effective.

MR. WELLS:

There was one major plus. TCG and Sun always have looked at operations in the same way, operating with a market strategy and not a product strategy.

MR. STRICKLAND:

You can't foresee all the problems—with loan portfolios for example. But you get the point where you expect the unexpected. However, nothing has come along to knock us out of the box. . . . One trouble in bringing two companies together is trying to submerge egos.

MR. WELLS:

For mergers to be successful, it is important to be able to relate to the new companies. If you think in those terms, things become relatively simple.

MR. STRICKLAND:

> Nobody has lost a job because of the merger.... All we had to do was organize the situations. People are too vital and too scarce to get rid of.

On the Situation Following the Original Merger and the Merger with Third National Corporation of Tennessee

MR. STRICKLAND:

> Well, the Georgia-Florida merger is done.... The direction of the new organization has been solidified.

MR. WELLS:

> All the mergers have been consistent; we are trying to be a viable organization.

MR. STRICKLAND:

> There were problems with the Tennessee mortgage and loan portfolios, but we have them on track.... The broad policies are set by the holding company. Meetings are held throughout the year; there are good communications between the banks.

Concerning the Direction of SunTrust.

MR. WELLS:

> We want to be in good markets, but we also must have a good position in those markets. In fact, I would rather be in a slower market as long as we have a good position in that market.... I think we'll go into other markets but in such a way so that we don't have to take our eyes off the overall organization.

LOCATION, LOCATION, LOCATION

SunTrust's secret weapon (though that hardly is the appropriate term) is its southeastern location.

Current estimates are that the U.S. economy will expand in the neighborhood of 2.5 percent in 1988; the Southeast should exceed that. There are several positive factors working in the region's favor:

• Continued population inflow will be an economic stimulant.
• Regional manufacturers should benefit from the lower value of the dollar in international trade.
• More balanced growth is expected between services and manufacturing.
• Aggregate economic output in the Southeast will continue to outperform the U.S. average and most other regions.
• Economic growth between metropolitan and less urbanized areas will tend to become more equalized.

But let's look at SunTrust's three primary locations.

Florida

The remarkable strength of the Florida economy is evident in virtually every measure of economic activity. Job gains, personal income growth and especially population increases have thrust Florida into the upper strata of state rankings. Over the course of the current business expansion (1982–1987), total personal income in Florida grew by 50 percent, compared with the U.S. rate of approximately 35 percent. Florida's labor market has averaged gains of over 200,000 jobs per year since 1982.

Between 1980 and 1987, more than two million new residents, or about 325,000 per year, moved into the state. Last year, Florida's total population passed the 12 million mark, a 3.1 percent increase over 1986. Florida edged out Illinois to become the fifth most populous state in the United States in 1986 and has now surpassed Pennsylvania to become fourth.

One of Florida's major attractions is its robust economy. The rate of new job creation of 4.5 percent per year is almost twice the national average. Employment is heavily weighted toward service-related businesses. Finance, insurance, and real estate all grew at a rate in excess of 4 percent in 1987. Although manufacturing remains a relatively small component in the total Florida economy, manufacturing jobs in Florida were being added at double the U.S. pace. Florida's unemployment rate, 5.0 percent, in mid-1988, has been consistently below the national average.

Construction has been vigorous throughout most of the past five-year expansion. Some slowdown has taken place since 1986, but this is a positive development since overbuilding in multi-unit structures and office buildings was evident.

SunTrust, through its Sun Banks group, is well-positioned in Florida with 20 banks, 315 banking locations and a market share of 12.3 percent of the state's bank deposits.

Georgia

The current period of business expansion has been favorable to Georgia. Since 1982 the primary measures of regional economic activity—employment growth and personal income gains—have placed Georgia in the forefront of national rankings. Georgia's strengths have been centered in the construction, trade, and service sectors. The state's pivotal location in the region, with Atlanta as the hub, has continued to contribute to very strong distribution and transportation activities. There has also been notable improvement in the manufacturing sector.

Personal income gains in Georgia have consistently exceeded the U.S. average over the course of the business cycle. The state ranked third in the country in personal income growth between late 1982 and mid-1987. Most of the vigorous growth in personal income stemmed from a strong labor market with the unemployment rate approximately 5.5 percent in 1987.

This mix of increasing job opportunities and rapid growth in personal income has attracted new residents from other parts of the region as well as the rest of the country.

Between 1980 and 1987, the state's population expanded by approximately 14 percent of 759,000 people, the fourth largest gain in the U.S.

The construction sector has clearly slowed. Over the course of 1987 jobs in construction were off by 2 to 3 percent, and there has been retrenchment in starts of new office buildings and multi-unit structures.

Georgia's job-producing dynamo is the 18-county Atlanta metropolitan market which has more than half of all jobs in the state. As U.S. manufacturing improves with more competitive labor unit costs and a depreciated dollar, Georgia should share in this growth.

Suntrust, through its Trust Company Banks, is well-positioned in Georgia with 18 banks and 182 banking locations. It holds a 16.1 percent market share of bank deposits.

Tennessee

As manufacturing becomes a major pillar of growth in the overall U.S. economy, Tennessee will derive special benefits. One-fourth of workers in the state are engaged in manufacturing, well above the national figure of 18.0 percent. Manufacturing in Tennessee is tilted toward high value-added products, such as chemicals, paper, and publishing. Although still in the developmental stages, a major world-class auto production industry is emerging along Tennessee's central corridor.

Since 1980, Tennessee's population growth has been slightly below the overall U.S. pace. In the years immediately ahead and into the 1990s, it is possible that the growth in population will be above the U.S. average as people are attracted to the central part of the state.

In 1987, Tennessee had one of the most active labor markets in the Southeast. Approximately 80,000 workers were added to payrolls, an increase of 4 percent from 1986. The recent surge in hiring activity, together with the personal income growth this represents, has brought greater prosperity to Tennessee. Between mid-1986 and mid-1987, Tennessee ranked among the ten top states in the U.S. based on personal income gains. Over the 1982–1987 period income growth in Tennessee has been 4.0 percent greater than the U.S. average. Last year personal income advances in the state were well over 7.0 percent, compared with a U.S. gain of 5.1 percent. Tennessee's unemployment rate has been decreasing from 1985–1986 levels and at present is 6.0 percent.

Third National Corporation, SunTrust's Tennessee subsidiary, serves the state through its group of 14 banks with 133 banking locations. These banks have a 14.4 percent market share of the state's bank deposits.

COCA-COLA, TOO

In 1919 Trust Company underwrote the first public offering of common stock of The Coca-Cola Company. The bank's commission was $110,000 of Coca-Cola stock.

Through stock dividends and splits, each original share of Coca-Cola is now 576 shares, giving SunTrust ownership of 6,033,312 shares. At year-end 1987, SunTrust's investment in Coca-Cola stock had a market value of $229.9 million.

To this day Coca-Cola's secret formula reposes in the vault at the Trust Company of Georgia's main office in Atlanta. Oh, yes, the formula for the new Coca-Cola flavor, introduced with much fanfare (and less public acceptance) a few years ago is also kept in the bank's vault.

FRAMING THE FUTURE

"As SunTrust continues to grow and do business in these competitive times, we felt the need to get all of our people and companies headed in a common direction from a strategic point of view," explains Bob Strickland, chairman and CEO. "Work began during the summer of 1986 to try to develop a corporate philosophy that could be used by all of our people."

SunTrust, with the assistance of the consulting firm of McKinsey and Company, began to develop this corporate ideology by conducting numerous interviews with managers and by analyzing the company's business. A broad cross section of SunTrust managers form Florida, Georgia, and Tennessee met to exchange ideas and discuss ways of implementing the philosophy.

After months of planning, a precisely worded statement of the company's corporate philosophy and objectives was developed to capture the spirit and goals of SunTrust. The written text was subjected to considerable editing and refinement to ensure that each word and phrase accurately described the company's aspirations. It summarizes how the company views its place in the financial services industry, both now and in the years ahead.

George Snelling, SunTrust executive vice president responsible for corporate development, coordinated the production of the Vision statement, and is charged with implementing its strategic planning process.

The major strategy in implementing the corporate philosophy includes continuing to develop a superior group of talented employees, increasing market share in those areas with greatest profit potential, capitalizing on operating economies, securing the lowest possible cost of external funding, and managing technology as efficiently as possible.

The Sun Trust Vision

MISSION: SunTrust Banks, Inc. will be a leading provider of high-value financial services. Our mission is to provide a high return to our shareholders by promoting the economic well-being of our customers and communities. We will combine the advantages of strong, focused, decentralized local management with financial, technological and capital markets power to achieve this mission.

OBJECTIVES: Our primary objective will be to operate sound financial institutions. This will benefit our customers, and rewards to our shareholders will flow from market recognition of our ability to remain sound while achieving high performance over time. Thus, we seek growth but will not sacrifice quality or profitability. Our aim is to achieve all three.

GEOGRAPHIC COVERAGE: We concentrate on customers with a material presence located within our region and also on others, including national and international concerns, to whom we can offer unique capabilities.

TARGET MARKETS: We seek to develop close, long-term relationships with customers who put a premium on high-quality, value-added service and superior professional attention. Our primary customer targets are successful, growing businesses, and institutions and individuals with above-average financial service needs. The emphasis placed on our primary markets will vary, depending on the size and nature of our communities. In addition, we will offer a basic level of service to all customers in our communities, ascertaining and assisting in meeting their credit needs. We also seek to serve other customer groups on a product-by-product basis when there is an opportunity for profit and when it does not conflict with our primary areas of emphasis.

SERVICES: We will offer financial services that satisfy the needs of our target markets and on which we can make an acceptable return at acceptable risk. Our success will depend heavily on our ability to understand these criteria better than our competitors and to act accordingly, regardless of near-term competitive moves. We will move aggressively to identify and exploit new opportunities for profit, although we anticipate our major sources of earnings will continue to be depository, lending, investment and asset management activities.

DELIVERY: We will utilize decentralized management to respond effectively to individual markets. We will strive to develop efficient delivery systems that enhance service quality to our target markets, expanding or contracting our facilities and deploying technology as conditions warrant.

It is this kind of planning and commitment to the organization that has brought SunTrust so far so soon—and will help insure progress in the years ahead.

SUNTRUST IS SHINING

That certainly is the picture one gets from the accompanying performance figures (Tables 2–1 and 2–2, pages 30–33.)

Last year was a very good year for this new super-regional. In fact, *American Banker's* annual survey of top banking companies ranked SunTrust Banks, Inc. first among regionals with assets over $20 billion. In addition, its market capitalization (Table 2–3, page 34) ranked sixth in the country, as of May 26, 1988, according to figures compiled by Keefe, Bruyette & Woods, Inc. And the other banks in the top ten are not bad neighbors to be keeping company with.

Based on past performance and the relative smoothness of the merger, it is fairly safe to say that the sun won't be setting anytime soon on SunTrust.

MERGING TWO BANKS WITH SKILL

The chairman of SunTrust banks, Bob Strickland, had this to say about mergers: "You can't foresee all the problems."

He is right, of course. But you can try to cover all bases and, in so doing, minimize the problems that do arise.

As the merging of banking organizations becomes increasingly more common, and the difficulties that arise in some mergers receive detailed publicity, one might think that any given merger, though not trouble-free, should develop more smoothly than would otherwise be the case.

Sad to say, that doesn't always happen. For one thing, the rules or roadmaps covering bank mergers, beyond the legal requirements, are often sketchy and, at times, nonexistent. Also, while there are a growing number of merger specialists, and they should be gaining in experience, they rarely operate uniformly since they each have their own priorities.

In addition, many banking organizations are bent on merger regardless of problems or potential problems. Consequently, they sometimes do not bother with all the details and simply move ahead with the corporate marriage.

In many merger situations, the overall benefits of a merger may be such that the problems, even serious ones, are accepted as part of the cost of merger, and dealt with when the time comes.

Still, the fewer surprises there are, the better. By and large, it is of considerable help to know where the problems are beforehand. Then advance measures can be taken to deal with them as soon as possible, or at least, the stage can be set for implementing solutions. Such preliminary efforts can actually reduce the time needed to put a solution in place, and thereby lower costs that may occur.

In the SunTrust situation, where there was a year to work things out (while waiting for regulatory approvals and the trigger dates in the applicable state laws), the basic sensitive areas—price, management placement or displacement, and organizational structure—were mostly settled prior to the effective date.

TABLE 2–1
Selected Financial Data (Dollars in millions execept per share data)

	For the Year Ended December 31					
	1987	1986	1985	1984	1983	1982
Interest and dividend income, taxable-equivalent	$ 2,295.9	$ 2,283.3	$ 2,174.7	$ 2,070.9	$ 1,495.1	$ 1,381.9
Interest expense	1,111.3	1,134.7	1,141.1	1,156.2	805.4	801.5
Net interest income	1,184.6	1,148.6	1,033.6	914.0	689.7	580.4
Provision for loan losses	143.4	151.9	96.3	68.0	47.0	45.7
Net interest income after provision for loan losses	1,041.2	996.7	937.3	846.7	642.7	534.7
Noninterest income	397.8	375.5	316.3	285.9	197.9	147.6
Noninterest expense	958.5	914.7	851.6	770.1	556.1	469.0
Income before income taxes	480.5	457.5	402.0	362.5	284.5	213.3
Taxable-equivalent adjustment	132.4	202.0	153.5	146.4	108.7	95.4
Provision for income taxes	65.3	13.3	32.8	24.1	21.8	0.1
Net income	$ 282.8	$ 242.2	$ 215.7	$ 192.0	$ 154.0	$ 117.8
Per common share:						
Net Income	$ 2.17	$ 1.83	$ 1.64	$ 1.47	$ 1.35	$ 1.08
Dividends declared	.65	.61	.56	.48	.39	.34
Total dividends declared:						
Preferred	.3	.8	1.0	1.1	.5	2.2
Common	84.4	75.0	68.6	56.8	41.7	34.0
Common dividend payout ratio	29.9%	31.1%	32.0%	29.7%	27.2%	29.4%
Averages for the year:						
Total assets	$24,502.8	$23,823.8	$21,066.1	$18,644.7	$13,919.7	$11,574.4
Earning assets	22,540.0	20,884.8	18,248.7	16,030.7	12,020.5	9,803.7
Loans	17,572.8	15,213.1	13,072.1	10,696.2	7,077.8	6,002.1
Deposits	21,017.8	19,227.1	17,113.6	15,096.5	10,945.8	8,843.6
Long-term debt	408.8	392.6	247.1	230.4	171.6	155.7
Common shareholders' equity	1,586.1	1,446.9	1,298.9	1,148.6	834.5	683.9

TABLE 2–1
Selected Financial Data (Dollars in millions execept per share data) (continued)

	For the Year Ended December 31					
	1987	1986	1985	1984	1983	1982
At December 31:						
Total assets	$27,187.9	$26,146.7	$24,434.6	$20,337.6	$17,957.0	$13,231.3
Earning assets	23,747.1	22,590.5	20,841.8	17,140.2	15,097.8	11,301.0
Loans	18,410.4	16,879.4	14,360.7	12,201.6	9,314.1	6,517.7
Deposits	22,493.3	21,284.0	18,967.8	16,610.9	14,281.2	10,070.7
Long-term debt	426.2	403.5	333.9	219.2	257.4	164.8
Common shareholders' equity	1,673.7	1,485.3	1,367.3	1,221.7	1,065.7	785.0
Average ratios:						
ROA	1.11%	1.02%	1.02%	1.03%	1.11%	1.02%
ROE	17.81	16.68	16.53	16.62	18.40	16.91
Net interest margin	5.26	5.50	5.66	5.71	5.74	5.92
Shareholders' equity to:						
Total Assets	6.23	6.12	6.22	6.22	6.02	6.10
Loans	9.05	9.58	10.03	10.84	11.85	11.77
Long-term debt to equity	25.72	26.93	18.85	19.88	20.47	22.05
Number of staffed banking offices	630	634	616	590	572	427
Number of full-time equivalent employees	20,047	19,711	19,473	18,868	17,735	13,984
Average common equivalent shares	130,389	131,673	130,951	129,912	114,148	106,807
Common stock price:*						
High	$ 27³/₄	$ 28	$ 20	—	—	—
Low	17	17¹/₄	15¹/₂	—	—	—
Close	18¹/₄	20	19¹/₈	—	—	—

* SunTrust's common stock began trading on the New York Stock Exchange on July 1, 1985. The common stock prices shown are market prices as reported by *The Wall Street Journal* adjusted to reflect the two-for-one stock split in the form of a 100% common stock dividend paid July 14, 1986.

TABLE 2–2
Selected Data by State (Dollars in millions)

	Sun Banks, Inc. Florida		Trust Company of Georgia		Third National Corporation Tennessee	
	1988	1987	1988	1987	1988	1987
For the first Quarter						
Net interest income (FTE)	$ 143.1	$ 137.1	$102.8	$ 94.9	$ 60.1	$ 55.7
Provision for loan losses	13.9	13.2	9.5	7.1	6.6	4.7
Noninterest income	47.7	46.6	37.6	35.0	17.5	16.4
Noninterest expense	125.9	116.6	77.6	71.2	46.0	45.0
Net income	32.8	30.9	35.7	32.1	14.9	12.5
Quarterly Averages						
Total assets	12,661	11,974	8,502	8,211	5,553	5,218
Earning assets	11,364	10,607	7,512	7,224	5,091	4,758
Loans	9,158	8,184	5,628	5,231	3,780	3,484
Deposits	11,025	10,383	6,305	5,852	4,703	4,321
Equity	838	738	695	592	412	371
At March 31						
Total assets	12,877	12,227	8,548	8,589	5,581	5,272
Earning assets	11,567	10,734	7,586	7,349	5,107	4,974
Loans	9,288	8,285	5,779	5,291	3,808	3,523
Reserve for loan losses	136	118	94	88	68	58
Deposits	11,196	10,690	6,450	6,019	4,655	4,397
Equity	848	748	702	599	419	376

TABLE 2-2
Selected Data by State (Dollars in millions) (continued)

	Sun Banks, Inc. Florida		Trust Company of Georgia		Third National Corporation Tennessee	
	1988	1987	1988	1987	1988	1987
Credit Quality						
Net domestic loan charge-offs	10.5	8.3	5.1	3.6	2.9	3.1
Loss on sale and net charge-off of Latin American loans charged against (credited to) reserve for loan losses	1.6	(.1)	1.5	—	—	(.2)
Reduction in Latin American loans	7.1	1.6	7.5	—	—	—
Nonperforming assets*	103.5	114.1	30.2	33.4	63.1	51.4
Ratios						
ROA†	1.04%	1.05%	1.69%	1.59%	1.08%	.97%
ROE†	15.72	16.96	20.65	22.00	14.55	13.63
Net interest margin†	5.06	5.24	5.50	5.33	4.75	4.75
Net domestic loan charge-offs to average loans†	.46	.41	.37	.28	.31	.37
Reserve/loans*	1.46	1.43	1.62	1.67	1.78	1.65
Reserve/nonperforming assets*	131.4	103.6	310.2	265.0	107.2	113.3

*At March 31.
†Annualized for the first quarter.

TABLE 2–3
Market Capitalization ($ in millions)*

1.	Citicorp	$7,311
2.	J. P. Morgan	6,435
3.	Security Pacific	3,834
4.	PNC Financial	3,690
5.	Wells Fargo	2,948
6.	SunTrust Banks	2,767
7.	BANC ONE Corporation	2,669
8.	Bankers Trust	2,583
9.	Fleet/Norstar	2,416
10.	First Union	2,369

*Priced as of May 26, 1988

Source: Keefe, Bruyette & Woods, Inc.

Within that time frame, for example, many of the operational problems with the two banks' data processing systems were addressed. There were two separate and different systems, although a lot of the software was the same. Both Sun Banks and the Trust Company of Georgia had their own operations subsidiaries. It was decided that the chief of the Sun Bank Service Corporation, Thomas Ash, would be head of the new bank's unit, Sun Trust Service Corporation, and that he would move to the new corporate headquarters in Atlanta.

Although many preparations could be made before the merger date on July 1, 1985, many of the specifics could not. Still, the reports indicate that the data processing merger has moved forward far more smoothly than had been hoped.

Perhaps the best advice is to study, as far as is feasible, the mergers which have already taken place. This includes both those that have worked satisfactorily and those that have not. Every solution is different, but there will be similarities; and the experience of others who have been through the process can, at the least, be enlightening and perhaps of real help.

One of the more difficult areas to determine where problems may arise is that dealing with personnel. In a department, for example, there can only be one boss. Who should be selected? Will the one not chosen accept second place? Will the policies and procedures used in the organization be accepted by those who previously followed other procedures?

Many of these things cannot be settled until after the merger is in effect. But spelling things out, working out obvious conflicts, and communicating fully the decisions that have been made certainly can help.

There will be problems in any merger situation, and some may be serious. But eventually they will be met and the issues resolved. The trick is to review the situation as fully as possible and not be surprised later on.

AN ACQUISITION THAT *REALLY* WORKED
The Wells Fargo Purchase of Crocker National—the Biggest Acquisition to Date—Has Been Almost Wildly Successful

Marriage is like life
in this—that it is
a field of battle, and
not a bed of roses.
—*Robert Louis Stevenson*

"This isn't a merger of equals; it's an acquisition, so don't expect to be dealt with as though we are partners." Those were the words of a Wells Fargo executive to a Crocker National Corporation loan officer shortly after Wells had purchased Crocker from London's Midland Band PLC.

The words were harsh, tough, hardly designed to generate any confidence or good feelings or even cooperation on the part of the Crocker official. At the same time, they painted a true picture of the situation. Moreover, to some extent, they reflected the approach being taken by the acquiring bank.

However, the Crocker people were, by and large, treated fairly. And the pragmatic manner in which Wells operates apparently did not antagonize the customers. As a result, the acquisition proceeded remarkably well, considering the size of the organizations and the logistics of melding together two statewide banking organizations.

CARL REICHARDT'S WELLS FARGO

If any bank is a symbol of California and the West, it is Wells Fargo. It was founded in 1852 during the California gold rush by Henry Wells and William Fargo.

36

When the banking and express opened its first office on Montgomery Street in San Francisco (not far from its current headquarters building on the same street), it contracted with independent stagecoach firms to move its express shipments. The stagecoach remains the trademark of this fast-moving institution, which many consider more than a super-regional and nearing money center bank status.

Carl E. Reichardt, a native Texan, graduated from the University of Southern California and has worked for California banks ever since. He joined Wells Fargo in 1970 as head of the Wells Fargo Mortgage and Equity Trust, a real estate investment trust. In 1978 he was named president of the bank. Then, when Richard Cooley left to be chief executive of troubled Seafirst in Seattle in late 1982, Reichardt was promoted to chairman and chief executive of Wells Fargo.

The change in management style from the cool Mr. Cooley could hardly have been more dramatic. Carl Reichardt is earthy, hard-nosed, brash, efficient. Now 56, he has moved Wells Fargo along in rather spectacular fashion since taking over the reins of the organization in 1983.

Few people knew much about Reichardt at the time. That is certainly not the case any more. In fact, Donald Crowley, bank stock analyst with Keefe, Bruyette & Woods, says Carl Reichardt "may be the best manager of a major bank today."

He has built much of the bank's progress upon a deregulation strategy devised in 1981 by himself, Cooley, and the present vice chairman, Robert Voss. That strategy included the downgrading of Wells Fargo's presence in U.S. corporate markets and concentrating instead mainly on a few core businesses in California which, Reichardt points out, is the sixth largest economy in the world. The bank currently concentrates its lending primarily in consumer loans, real estate, and the middle market companies with annual sales between $5 and $100 million.

Today Wells Fargo is the second largest real estate and construction lender in the country, the second largest agricultural lender, and through Wells Fargo Investment Advisors, it runs the sixth largest index fund in the United States.

Last year Wells bought Bank of America's personal trust division. Reichardt considers this a core business of his bank, and many observers consider Wells' personal trust operation to be the biggest in the country.

The strategic plan has resulted in the closing of many of the bank's European and other overseas offices, particularly in the Middle East and Africa. However, Mr. Reichardt says, "Our future overseas operations will be in the Pacific Rim because of California's strong trading relationships in that part of the world." Referring to the bank's Latin American debt exposure, he noted that "we will also continue to do business in Latin America because we don't have much choice."

But more than anything, Carl Reichardt's Wells Fargo is a bank that is driven by an emphasis on cost control. Shortly after he took charge, executive salaries were frozen, the corporate jet was sold, convention attendance was scaled back.

These moves, of course, were merely surface steps. The real cost cutting has been in operations. Staff was reduced, branches have been consolidated or closed. Data processing functions were merged into regional centers, automatic teller machines (ATMs) have replaced hundreds of live tellers throughout the system. As John Grundhofer, the executive vice president and senior executive for southern California, puts it: "We are on a permanent diet of cost control and expense control because we are very bottom-line oriented."

While under Reichardt's direction, the bank has made great strides (see Table 2–4). But the move that has really put Wells Fargo—and Carl Reichardt—on the banking map both here in the United States and abroad was its acquisition of Crocker National Corporation.

THE CROCKER ACQUISITION

Crocker National had been struggling for years and had become a burden to its British owners. Midland acquired Crocker in 1981 and completed the purchase of all its stock in 1985. During much of that time, Crocker sustained substantial foreign and agricultural loan losses.

Actually, when Wells announced its intention to buy its neighbor across the street in San Francisco in early February,

TABLE 2-4
Six-Year Summary of Selected Financial Data (in millions)*

	1986	1985	1984	1983	1982	1981	Change 1986/1985	Five-year compound growth rate
Income Statement								
Net interest income	$1,608.9	$1,220.2	$1,069.5	$915.0	$821.9	$731.0	32%	17%
Provision for loan losses	361.7	371.8	194.6	121.1	115.4	63.4	(3)	42
Noninterest income	459.6	395.7	270.6	279.5	293.9	231.3	16	15
Noninterest expense	1,315.2	943.8	886.6	843.7	836.6	743.5	39	12
Net income	273.5	190.0	169.3	154.9	138.6	124.0	44	17
Per common share†								
Net Income	5.03	4.15	3.42	3.01	2.90	2.66	21	14
Dividends declared	1.41	1.24	1.08	.99	.96	.96	14	8
Balance Sheet								
Loans	$36,771.1	$24,614.2	$22,893.9	$20,267.6	$19,768.5	$17,977.7	49%	15%
Allowance for loan losses	734.0	417.5	260.3	199.6	190.5	153.1	76	37
Assets	44,577.1	29,429.4	28,184.1	27,017.6	24,814.0	23,219.2	51	14
Senior debt	2,019.1	2,129.7	1,708.6	1,493.7	1,335.2	968.4	(5)	16
Subordinated debt	2,392.4	2,056.5	1,011.7	38.8	38.8	38.8	16	128
Stockholders' equity	2,342.7	1,458.0	1,343.7	1,347.8	1,100.4	1020.9	61	18

*Reflects the acquisition of Crocker National Corporation beginning June 1, 1986.
†Adjusted to reflect the 2-for-1 common stock split.

Crocker was in its best shape in years. Its foreign operations had been absorbed by Midland, and many of its bad loans were written off. The bank had assets of $19.2 billion with 1985 income totalling $38 million (following a disastrous 1984 when it lost $324 million).

Wells Fargo was interested in Crocker for, among other things, it 319 branch network, much of it in fast-growing southern California where Wells was relatively weak.

"We are especially enthusiastic about southern California; the dynamics are outstanding," Reichardt points out. "If it were a separate economy, it would be the tenth largest in the world."

After doing a lot of analysis, the Wells Fargo chairman says, "It became obvious to us that in order to make a dent in southern California with anything like economies of scale, an acquisition was the way to go."

Speaking to a group of San Franciso stock analysts several months after the Crocker acquisition, Mr. Reichardt made the following remarks:

> We talked to the Midland people, and they were in the process of doing some long-range planning themselves. As you know, the Crocker acquisition had not gone particularly well for them. They were anticipating the "big bang" in the United Kingdom and had made a strategic decision that they should really focus on protecting their home market. The capital that they had here was badly needed back home. . . .
>
> The discussions with Midland were straightforward. They told us what the price would be and that it was not negotiable. We told them that the bank had to be clean. We could create enough problems for ourselves—we didn't intend to buy a bank that was burdened with international debt or the other serious problems that you read about in the paper. . . .
>
> So it was a very complicated deal even though it was, and still is, the largest domestic bank merger. And it was for cash. . . .
>
> As you know, we had to go to the capital markets. One of the things the Federal Reserve was insistent upon was that they did not want our capital ratios to deteriorate, which is understandable. We agreed to issue both common and preferred stock. Fortunately, the market was going in our direction and it worked quite well. . . .

We submitted our application in February, and it was approved April 30, which is very fast for something of this magnitude. The regulators were supportive; they handled things in an expeditious fashion. . . .

Paul Hazen [president of Wells Fargo] and I were involved in the analysis of the loan portfolio, and we felt comfortable that in buying Crocker, what we saw was what we were getting. And I can tell you now, several months into it, that portfolio was, in fact, clean. . . .

So we bought a bank that make a lot of sense for Wells Fargo.

After the analysis we tried to explain to people who were interested, those who held our stock for instance, that this was an exercise in expense control. There was no magic here. No alchemy occurred. It was purely and simply a method of rationalizing redundant systems.

Carl Reichardt gives Hazen full credit for negotiating the Crocker deal. Paul Hazen has worked closely with Reichardt for many years—they were at Union Bank before joining Wells.

The acquisition was a bargain. Wells paid book value for Crocker. Many, if not most, banks are sold at two or three times book. Without question, the purchase price—$1.1 billion—has turned out to be money well spent.

AFTER THE ACQUISITION

Wells Fargo went into its merger/acquisition of Crocker with well-thought-out plans and procedures. The objective was to leave as little as possible to chance and to move everything along on a fast-moving course. The plans called for the completion of all phases within 18 months. By any measure the acquisition was completed ahead of that admittedly tight schedule.

This was not what the critics (including more than a few competitors) either wanted or expected. Even some bank stock analysts expected Wells to stumble if not fail in the Crocker acquisition process.

But the dire predictions never happened. Sure, there were

problems, although they did little to slow things down. If fact, the arrangements have gone more smoothly than even the most optimistic supporters expected.

Jack L. Hancock, a Wells Fargo senior vice president who is in charge of computer systems, was put in charge of a team to work out the details of the acquisition to be followed once the deal was done. Three basic rules were developed, covering

- Customer retention and acquisition.
- Successful handling of internal personnel problems.
- Successful system integrations.

Customer Retention

The branch offices of the two institutions, totalling 613, have now been reduced to about 450. Customer loss has proven to be quite low. One reason may have been that some of the Crocker branches were redundant, with Wells offices already in the same locations, so that account transfers required little effort and almost no inconvenience.

Vice Chairman William Zuendt, who is in charge of Wells Fargo's retail banking group, is credited with much of the success in merging retail operations. He insisted that Crocker customers not be inconvenienced by the details of the changeover.

This was accomplished in several ways. Letters were sent to all Crocker customers advising them that, among other things, they did not have to order new checks. They were also given a special phone number to call for answers to their questions.

In addition, the two banks' credit card operations were combined within six months following the acquisition approval.

Personnel

This may have been the stickiest part of the plan. The move generated some bad publicity as the quote that started this chapter (and was published in *The Wall Street Journal*) attests. There certainly were problems, and a number of Crocker people felt abused by how the acquisition was handled.

Still, those who were displaced should not have been surprised by the personnel reductions that took place. . . .

"At a press conference," Mr. Reichardt explains, "I announced that one of our objectives was to reduce the number of employees. I believe it is more humane to get it over instead of nibbling away," he told us two years after the actual acquisition. Also, he pointed out, "a lot of people were let go through attrition."

By the end of 1986, over 3,000 employees had been pared from the combined work force of 24,000. It has now been trimmed by 4,500 people, including a number of Wells employees.

A report in the *American Banker* in October 1986 noted that employee turnover at acquired institutions usually multiplies. But at Crocker it actually declined from 25 percent just before announcement of the acquisition to 5 percent afterwards.

Stephen Enna, a Wells Fargo senior vice-president in charge of human resources, said considerable time was spent making sure that people were treated fairly. "To the extent you can inform employees of their status and the policies that affect them," he commented, "you'll minimize disruption in the workplace."

Reports to the contrary, Crocker employees who were displaced received at least 30 days' notice and were given severance pay. In addition, workshops were held to assist them in finding other jobs.

System Integration

Within three months the two banks' ATM systems were merged into Wells Fargo's "Express Stop" machines. This is now the nation's second largest 24-hour ATM network.

According to Mr. Reichardt, all the Wells branches and most of the Crocker branches have at least two ATMs on separate phone systems and on separate computer systems. Moreover, he said "We are running over 100 million transactions every month."

Crocker had some good systems, Reichardt observed, and "some were better than ours. However, we decided to move theirs into ours."

Because things did move well, the bank was able to consolidate the credit card and data processing centers about a year after the acquisition.

ECONOMIES OF SCALE AND OTHER BENEFITS

"Crocker and Wells were very similar," the Wells Fargo chairman said. As a result, the acquisition "gave us an opportunity to experience economies of scale." In fact, he added, "in almost every case we did better than we thought we could do."

It wasn't long before $10 million a month was cut from Crocker's expense base. This translates into a substantial savings of $240 million a year.

The acquisition has resulted in an expanded base which Wells Fargo is already capitalizing on. The bank increased its market share of total deposits in California from 5 percent to approximately 9 percent. It now has nearly 16 percent of the market in northern California and about 4 percent in the southern part of the state.

Not only that, Mr. Reichardt said somewhat ironically, the bank was able to "almost double our size with no added foreign loans." He was referring, of course, to the nonperforming Latin American loans that reduced Wells Fargo's last year's earnings (see Table 2–5).

An interesting postscript to the acquisition came in December 1986, when employees received a letter from Chairman Reichardt and President Hazen thanking them for their efforts during the merger. Many employees had been putting in extra time to get the two banks operating as one.

"The consolidation is right on schedule," the two executives wrote, "and our cost savings are better than we expected. To thank you for your hard work, we want you to take a break."

TABLE 2–5

Wells Fargo & Company and Subsidiaries—1987 Earnings Highlights (in millions, except per share data)

	Quarter Ended			% Change from 12/31/87	
	12/31/87	9/30/87	12/31/87	9/30/87	12/31/86
Net income	$111.2	$155.0	$78.4	(28)%	42%
Per common share					
Net income	1.95	2.77	1.36	(30)	43
Dividends declared	.50	.39	.39	28	28
Average common shares outstanding (in thousands)	53,735	53,981	53,629	–	–

	Year ended 12/31		% Change
	1987	1986	
Net income	$50.8	$273.5	(81)%
Per common share			
Net income	.52	5.03	(90)%
Dividends declared	1.67	1.41	18
Average common shares outstanding (in thousands)	53,805	50,875	6

	Quarter Ended			% Change from 12/31/87	
	12/31/87	9/30/87	12/31/87	9/30/87	12/31/86
Loans	$36,791.1	$36,330.3	$36,771.1	1%	–%
Allowance for loan losses	1,357.2	1,299.6	734.0	4	85
Assets	44,183.3	45,145.0	44,577.1	(2)	(1)
Stockholders' equity	2,247.6	2,221.6	2,342.7	1	(4)
Primary Capital	4,046.1	3,965.7	3,551.2	2	14
Total capital	6,369.5	6,296.7	6,093.7	1	5

The employees received a three-part package that included:

• A paid holiday and a coffee mug.
• A $100 bonus (*not* in lieu of a Christmas bonus).
• An extra week of paid vacation.

Incidentally, both Wells Fargo and former Crocker employees received the package.

A STOCK ANALYST'S FAVORITE

The aggressive performance of Wells Fargo in recent years under Carl Reichardt's leadership has made the banking company a favorite of bank stock analysts as the following examples indicate:

> Fox Pitt, Kelton, Inc.
> August 20, 1987
>   We rate Wells Fargo a BUY as we consider the shares undervalued based on its low price/earnings ratio. We expect earnings momentum to remain strong as the company continues to consolidate the Crocker National acquisition, contain expense growth, and improve credit quality.
>   Expenses have been well contained during the past several years, leading to the earnings improvement evidenced during this period. Net non-interest expenses as a percentage of average assets have been reduced dramatically. Management remains committed to the policy of cost containment as it strives to achieve its higher financial goals.
>   Wells Fargo has developed expertise in several areas, including real estate and middle market lending, retail banking, financing corporate recapitalizations, and trust (including a newly acquired addition to the consumer trust business). At the same time areas that do not meet corporate goals are divested, such as the commercial finance subsidiary whose sale is pending.
>
> Paine Webber
> November 9, 1987.
>   We believe Wells Fargo's stock can outperform the market in the period ahead because:
>
> • Underlying earnings trends are stronger than at most companies because of continued aggressive cost control and moderate revenue growth.
> • The stock is very cheap compared to the market and its own historic valuation range.
>
> Shearson Lehman Hutton
> May 3, 1988
>   We continue to aggressively recommend purchase of Wells Fargo's shares and retain a 2/1 investment ranking on the stock. Our

recommendation, which has been based in part on the company's strong earnings momentum, is reinforced by first quarter 1988 results, which saw profits surpass even our aggressive forecast. Wells Fargo earned a record high $2.15 per share, an impressive 58.1 percent above the year-earlier level and $0.20 better than earnings for the previous three months. Earnings benefited not only from a stronger than expected 4.76 percent net interest margin but also from reduced loan losses, which have permitted the company to maintain non-LDC loan loss provisioning at the $75 million per quarter pace established in the second half of 1987. At the same time expenses have remained under remarkable control, demonstrating a 2.3 percent year-to-year decline.

We are retaining our full year 1988 earnings estimate of $8.70 per share, which has been well above general Street forecasts. We think that this figure, which would represent a 30 percent increase from 1987 (excluding special LDC loan loss provisioning), is achievable even though net interest margins are likely to contract later in the year. Furthermore, we believe that as investors begin to recognize Wells Fargo's earnings growth potential, the shares have substantial potential to be revalued upward and that the shares will be among the best performing regional bank stocks.

WHERE NOW, WELLS FARGO?

With about $45 billion in assets, Wells Fargo is now the third largest bank in California and the third biggest in the United States.

Earlier this year it acquired Barclays Bank of California. The purchase price of $125 million, Mr. Reichardt notes, classifies the purchase as "a little" acquisition. It also adds 50 branches, $1.3 billion in assets, and further increases Wells' retail presence in California. Also, Reichardt says, the acquisition adds $230 million in credit card business "at really no additional cost."

Wells Fargo may be poised for more and bigger acquisitions. At one time Carl Reichardt's goal was to overtake long-time rival Security Pacific. By the time you read this book, Wells may have already accomplished this feat.

That leaves only Bank of America in California to overtake.

DOING AN ACQUISITION RIGHT

The Wells Fargo acquisition of Crocker bank may have been the most successful large acquisition ever accomplished, and from all sorts of angles. So there certainly are lessons to be learned from how things were handled. Still, there were problems, most particularly the negative publicity.

Could the bad publicity have been eliminated? Probably not completely, although it might have been minimized with greater communications and instructions from Wells' management to its staff people who would be dealing with Crocker personnel.

By and large, however, Wells Fargo did most things right. Since this was an acquisition, of course, there was less need to try to take the best of both banks and merge things together. But merger or acquisition, advance planning is essential and this is what Wells did very well, indeed,

Goals were set and plans were devised to reach those goals. Timetables were established and plans were meshed to coincide with the timetables. Any acquisition will go better if those few steps are taken.

What Wells did could be likened to a full-court press in basketball. All positions were covered and everyone was enlisted in making the acquisition work.

Particular attention must be given to the customers of the acquired bank. This was one of the things that Wells did best. It tried to inconvenience those customers as little as possible and exerted extra effort to answer their questions and deal with their concerns.

Carl Reichardt observed that Wells and Crocker were very similar, particularly in relation to their customer bases. This did make the retention of customers easier perhaps, but they still should not be taken for granted.

The absorption of employees into the surviving organization was the most difficult part of this acquisition and likely will be in any acquisition. Some people will be terminated, and this should be handled as humanely as possible. In most instances senior officers from the acquired bank won't be needed. About 1,500 Crocker management people were released right after the acquisition. This was a shock that might have been tempered by delay, but, in the long run, would releasing them later have been any more humane?

In any merger or acquisition, some people won't like the management style—or the procedures or the policies—of the new or acquiring bank. They will be dissatisfied or won't fit in. This is a fact of corporate life and must be faced. And no amount of planning will change the reality of this.

Wells moved as fast as it could to cut costs, join systems, and realize any economies of scale possible. By doing this, and doing it successfully, it benefitted the organization and the stockholders.

If a bank can accomplish this, it certainly is moving in the right direction.

CHAPTER 3

EMPHASIZING COMMUNITY RELATIONS
National Community Bank Shows What Being a Good Neighbor Is All About

Goodness is the only investment
that never fails.
—*Henry David Thoreau*

Most banks get involved in community relations activities to some extent; few, however, are as committed to the concept as is National Community Bank, a $3 billion institution headquartered in Maywood, New Jersey, about 20 miles from New York City.

This emphasis on community relations has come about because the president of the bank, Robert M. Kossick, believes it is an obligation of the bank to be a true corporate citizen of the communities it serves. He also believes it is good business.

Mr. Kossick is right on both counts. Banks, as responsible members of a community—and the community could be a town, a county, even a state—should help support the people and the businesses in that community. This helps the community to prosper and be a better place in which to live. And a prosperous, healthy community will, in turn, help the bank grow and prosper.

As Tables 3–1 through 3–4 and Figures 3–1 and 3–2 illustrate, National Community Bank has been performing exceptionally well.

When Bob Kossick came to NCB as President in 19 9, the

TABLE 3–1
**Return-on-Assets (ROA) & Return-on-Equity (ROE) NCB vs. Industry
"Composite" (Average) Bank***

	1982	1983	1984	1985	1986	1987
NCB-ROA	1.01	1.01	1.09	1.22	1.22	1.24
Average Bank-ROA	.68	.67	.67	.66	.69	(.07)
NCB-ROE	14.92	15.42	17.73	20.39	21.50	22.75
Average Bank-ROE	13.21	13.35	13.04	14.16	14.18	(1.17)

*Source of Data: Keefe, Bruyette & Woods, Inc.

bank had 49 offices. It was located in six counties of the state, and had $1.056 billion in assets. Today, the bank has 96 branch offices (plus 12 more in various stages of completion), serves 12 of New Jersey's 21 counties, and (as of June 30, 1988) has assets totalling $3,339 billion.

This solid, near-spectacular growth is not just because the bank has been such a good community citizen during the past nine years. A bank won't perform well without good management, products, and service; intelligent strategic plans; effective marketing efforts; and a host of other factors. Obviously, National Community has all of the above.

TABLE 3–2
NCB Earnings & Stock Performance

	1982	1983	1984	1985	1986	1987
			Earnings			
Total (In millions)	$ 12.04	$ 13.53	$ 17.08	$ 22.26	$ 27.45	$ 34.53
Per Share (In dollars)	$ 1.18	$ 1.33	$ 1.67	$ 2.16	$ 2.66	$ 3.34
Shares Outstanding (In millions)	10.21	10.21	10.25	10.31	10.32	10.35
			Value			
Stock Price (Offered)	$ 7.00	$ 10.88	$ 12.25	$ 24.50	$ 28.50	$ 37.50
Bank Total Share Value (In millions)	$ 71.50	$111.00	$125.60	$253.30	$294.12	$388.99
Book Value	$ 8.33	$ 9.02	$ 10.02	$ 11.45	$ 13.38	$ 15.76

TABLE 3–3
Growth Rates NCB vs. Peer Banks in Nation*

Growth	1982	1983	1984	1985	1986	1987
Assets-NCB	10%	15%	16%	19%	35%	15%
Assets-Peers	10%	11%	12%	13%	13%	7%

*Source of Data: Comptroller of the Currency Uniform Bank Performance Reports

However, and without question, NCB's growth has been enhanced by its community relations activities.

REPORTING ON COMMUNITY RELATIONS

In its annual reports, NCB usually can be expected to include two features which, in a way, complement each other: a "Customer's Showcase," which is pages of photos of some of the bank's corporate and government customers; and "Community Service," two pages of photos of community and business organization events with which the president has been personally involved. In the 1987 annual report, for example, are photographs of Mr. Kossick

- Chairing a benefit for the John Harms Center for the Performing Arts, Englewood, and chatting with the evening's honoree, Charles Osgood of CBS.
- With honoree David A. (Sonny) Werblin at a benefit for the Fund for Educational Advancement.
- With honorees, the Visceglia brothers, at the Thomas A. Edison Council Boy Scouts of America luncheon.
- Chairing, for the second consecutive year, the Annual Golf and Tennis Outing for Felician College, Lodi, pictured with Sister Theresa Mary Martin, president of the college.
- As past honoree at the Columbian Foundation Annual Ball, with Senator Frank Lautenberg and the 1987 honoree.

TABLE 3–4
Financial Highlights

	1986 (In thousands of dollars)	1987	% Change 1986–1987
I. Earnings			
Net Income	$ 27,446	$ 34,534	26%
II. Resources			
Assets	$2,748,370	$3,153,051	15%
Loans	1,787,731	2,335,802	31%
Deposits	2,435,807	2,691,373	10%
Savings Deposits	1,050,063	1,209,477	15%
Shareholders' Equity	138,242	163,513	18%
III. Performance			
Return on Average Assets	1.22%	1.24%	
Return on Average Equity	21.50%	22.75%	
IV. Shareholder perspective			
Net Income Per Share	$ 2.66	$ 3.34	26%
Dividends Declared	.78	.96	23%
Shareholders' Equity (Book Value)	13.38	15.76	18%
Stock Price—Asked	28.50	37.50	32%
V. Bank's operating franchise			
Number of Counties Served	11	12	
Number of Bank Branches	81	96	
Number of Employees	1745	1958	

- Addressing the Industrial and Commercial Real Estate Women of New Jersey.
- Being recognized as Businessman of the Year by the Meadowlands Chamber of Commerce.
- Chairing a dinner to raise money for the West Hudson Council for the Handicapped.
- At the Bergen County Boy Scout luncheon honoring NCB chairman Fairleigh S. Dickinson
- Helping to raise $500,000 for the Northwest Bergen/Rampo Valley Chapter, American Red Cross.
- As Chairman of the 25th Anniversary Dinner for the Monmouth Council of Girl Scouts, pictured with Mary Little Parell, N.J. State Commissioner of Banking.

FIGURE 3–1
NCB's Total Size (in billions)

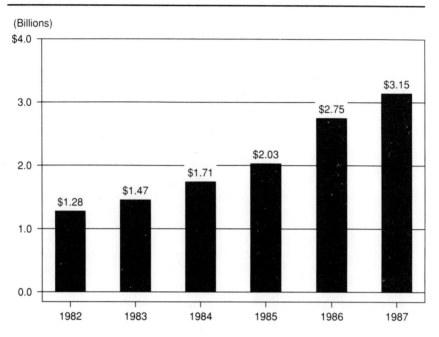

- As chairman of the First Annual Golf and Tennis Outing for St. Peter's Hospital, Middlesex County.
- Accepting an award on behalf of National Community Bank for the U.S. Small Business Administration.
- Presenting a check to the West Bergen Mental Health Center.

That is an extensive list, but it only touches on some of the community relations activities Kossick personally is involved with during the course of a year. He is quoted as saying that his life is the bank:

> At nighttime, we are involved in two particular types of activities for the bank. We do an awful lot of business development work wherein we get together with our best prospects and our best existing clients at my home for personal dinners. Secondly, we probably do more in the form of heading up major fund raisers for various entities within the state. . . .

FIGURE 3–2
Earnings (in millions)

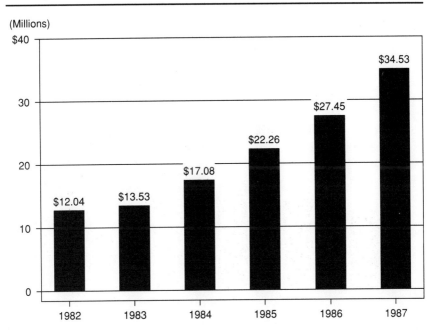

(Millions)

Few chief executives of banks devote the kind of time Bob Kossick does in community activities. He reaps a considerable amount of personal publicity for these efforts, certainly. But he believes this visibility is important since he is not just Robert Kossick, citizen, but the president of a National Community Bank. And this kind of publicity reflects most favorably on the bank.

AN ORGANIZATION-WIDE EFFORT

Community relations activities at National Community Bank, it must be pointed out, is not a one-man show. First Senior Vice President Arthur C. Ramirez, who oversees NCB's community support programs, notes that the bank has nine regions in the state, each composed of clusters of 12 banks. Management personnel in each of those regions are advised to take a high profile role in the area—get on boards of community and nonprofit groups, become involved in fund raising, take leadership positions wherever possible.

If a cause is large enough, the headquarter officers will become involved. For example, if an organization wishes to issue a fund-raising journal at a dinner, the bank will help to design it and print it (in the bank's print shop) at no cost to the organization.

We asked Mr. Ramirez for a list of some of the organizations with which National Community has been involved during the first half of 1988. The following includes only those groups that have been helped from the headquarters office.

- Girl Scout Council of Bergen County
- South Jersey Cancer Fund
- American Red Cross
- Ridgewood High School Football
- Township of Randolph
- League of Women Voters
- Boy Scouts of America/Bergen
- William Carlos Williams Center
- Tuxedo Park School
- National Coalition of 100 Black Women
- Fund for Educational Advancement
- The Graham-Windham Foundation
- West Hudson Council for the Handicapped
- Hackensack Hospital
- Felician College
- The John Harms Center for the Arts
- The Health and Welfare Council of Bergen County

That is a sizeable list, yet it merely scratches the surface of what National Community does on a bank-wide basis.

My family and I just so happen to live in Bergen County, in the northern part of New Jersey. National Community Bank has a fine reputation as a strong supporter of community groups in the area.

Ruth Miller, who is president of the Girl Scout Council of Bergen County, said that National Community has been most supportive of the Council. "Last year," she noted, "we issued a special newspaper commemorating the 75th anniversary of the Girl Scouts. National Community Bank not only printed but mailed or had inserted in newspapers 125,000 copies of our publication."

She said the bank is currently printing 5,000 copies of *The Source*, the Council's program booklet on goals and functions for adult leaders.

In addition, she mentioned that NCB printed and supplied the graphics for an 80-page booklet, *Help When You Need It*, a guide to community services for women and families that was published by the Health and Welfare Council (H&WC) of Bergen County. H & WC is distributing 25,000 copies.

It was her comments that led us to National Community as the subject bank for this chapter. Also, it should be noted, neither my family nor I bank at National Community—not for any reason but that another bank is more convenient.

The fact remains that National Community Bank, under the dynamic leadership of Robert Kossick, is doing one terrific job in the area of community relations. And along the way, the bank has become one of the top performing financial institutions in the country.

COMMUNITY RELATIONS CONCEPTS

We know of no bank in the country that is not, in some way, involved in community relations activities. It may well be a necessity for survival, if not for success. Any bank that turned down too many requests for assistance from community groups would soon find out how much the people in that community care about groups and the work they do.

At the same time, there does seem to be a diminishing of this aspect of the banking business as banks grow and control shifts away from local communities. After all, not too many large banks are quite as decentralized as is Barnett Banks (see Chapter 6).

That is not to say that big banks do not get involved in community relations activities, although more attention (and money) may be given to broader-based activities. And, certainly, gifts are probably dispensed from the headquarters office and not at the local level. Certainly, the president of a large bank, operating over much of a state or across several states, is unlikely to chair a dinner of a community "Y" or scout council.

That's not the way National Community Bank does it, and it could hardly be described as a small bank. The results of its emphasis on community relations have produced a strong, warm, positive feeling about the bank, even though many of its efforts receive little or no publicity.

NCB does not have a written policy covering how it deals with community relations; perhaps one is unnecessary, since the policy is to purposefully communicated from the top to the rest of the bank. However, it may be a good idea to formulate a community relations policy that is then made known to all bank personnel.

Here is one such policy, formulated by Frazier Seitel in his book, *The Practice of Public Relations*, published by Charles E. Merrill Publishing Co., Columbus, Ohio. His suggestions are particularly appropriate since his experience has been with a bank; he currently is vice president and director of public relations with the Chase Manhattan Bank.

> To commit a reasonable portion of our human and financial resources to improving the quality of life of our various publics, giving priority to those areas where our special competence can make a significant contribution and those areas having the most direct, immediate effect on the consumer of our services.
>
> To accumulate and maintain a body of knowledge that represents the current state of the art in social responsibility, including an annual inventory of our current activities that help improve the quality of life.
>
> Using our continuous research and criteria as a base, to recommend those specific programs with which the company can expect to most successfully achieve its objective.
>
> To establish machinery for management review and program maintenance. An ad hoc committee has been appointed by the president, which will provide review and maintenance, coordinate gifts and contributions policies, and recommend new programs to senior management.

Community groups are almost always in need of money, and donating funds is an obvious means for a bank to show its support.   But a bank—or any business, for that matter, can provide support in may other ways which may, in some instances, provide as much or more assistance. What National Community Bank does is an excellent role model.

PART 2

EFFECTIVE OPERATIONAL CONTROL

Without some kind of controls in place, a bank could get into big trouble—and many have. Of course, a bank could get into trouble even with controls, particularly if the controls are inadequate or are not properly enforced—and many have. Still, controls do limit abuses, set directions, encourage the acceptance of rules, focus innovative activities, and enhance the possibility of profitability.

Controls, it would seem, are well worth any effort required to develop and put them into effect.

With banking—really, the entire financial services industry—so complex and dynamic, operations could quickly get out of hand without controls. And, with things moving so rapidly these days, and with competitive forces so strong, the lack of effective control procedures could be disastrous for a bank, or several banks. . .or even for the industry itself.

Again, the Penn Square debacle is a near perfect example (as well as a loud and clear warning) of what absolutely awful results can come from situations that are allowed to get out of control.

If adequate procedures had been followed at that Oklahoma City bank, it might still be open for business today. If adequate procedures and policies existed and were followed, Continental Illinois might still be one of the premier banking companies in the country. If proper procedures were followed at Seafirst, it might never have become a unit of BankAmerica. And if controls had been effective at Michigan National Corporation, the first chapter in this book probably would have profiled a different bank and another chief executive.

Each of the chapters in this section illustrates different types of control: Fleet/Norstar, dealing with commercial lending, addresses some of the kinds of problems associated with Penn Square and how they could have been handled; First Wisconsin shows how controlled creativity can keep technology from taking charge, or at least getting out of hand; and Barnett Banks illustrates the importance of controls and procedures in helping to keep decentralized operations on the right track.

There are many other procedures that banks must have in place to keep their operations under control. The control areas in this section have been selected to show the range of controls utilized in banking, and how, when properly designed and utilized, they can accomplish so much.

CHAPTER 4

MANAGING CREDIT RISK
Fleet/Norstar Is Doing It—and on a Regionwide Basis, Too.

"How long have you been
a lending officer?"
"Forty years."
"How many bad loans have
you made?"
"None."
"You're fired."
—*Paul S. Nadler*

Fleet/Norstar Financial Group has received a great deal of attention, mostly favorable, over the past few years.

And rightly so. The two organizations have been performing well, expanding in specific areas as they have moved across state borders and throughout the country.

Much of the attention has been focused on Fleet's chief executive (who will become CEO of the merged organization in 1989), J. Terrence Murray. Brash and dynamic, Murray has been directing his organization with great skill, making the most of reciprocal interstate banking laws in New England and other states.

But one aspect of Fleet—and now Fleet/Norstar—that has received scant attention, yet is one of the pillars upon which the institution has been able to sustain its success, is the professional and innovative manner in which its commercial lending operations have been managed.

THE DEPTH AND BREADTH OF CORPORATE BANKING

Fleet/Norstar commercial lenders aim principally at the small-to-medium-sized companies, or the middle market. These firms account for the largest share of its business. Commercial loan growth in the New York State Banking Group was strong in 1987, with outstanding loans reaching a record level of $3.3 billion at year-end. Gross income, including fees, grew over the prior year, reflecting increased volume and a higher average prime rate.

Although the New York group's commercial loan portfolio is well-diversified, its four banks have developed an expertise in lending to highway and bridge contractors and allied firms such as heavy equipment dealers and concrete, asphalt, and aggregate materials suppliers. Other lending specialties include computer leasing companies and the wholesale and retail food industry.

The quality of the commercial loan portfolio continues to be satisfactory. And the low level of net chargeoffs and nonperforming loans attests to the banks' commitment to sound lending practices.

Within the New England Banking Group, earnings of Fleet National Bank's Commercial Lending Division were up more than 50 percent last year (excluding the Latin American loan provision—yes, another bank caught with its LDC loans down). This reflects the strong performances by the communications, precious metals, Rhode Island, Southeastern New England, and financial institutions lending groups. The Division's loan portfolio totalled $1.7 billion at year-end, an 18 percent increase over 1986.

The Communications Group doubled its earnings and expanded its portfolio by over 40 percent. Over the years, Fleet has achieved a reputation as a high-quality lender in the communications industry.

The Rhode Island and Southeastern New England commercial lending groups recorded record years, aided by a highly favorable economy in the area.

The New England Banking Group introduced an innovative

new product in 1987. Fleet Business Line, a preapproved line of credit for small businesses, had loans outstanding of approximately $25 million at the end of the year. The group's total portfolio exceeded $800 million.

Merrill/Norstar Bank in Maine began the partnership with a combined commercial loan portfolio of $525 million. New loan growth during the year was $66 million, an indicator that both banks boosted their market share. Commercial banking net income at United Bank in Connecticut has increased substantially, with its commercial loan portfolio at $862 million at the end of the year, up 18 percent over 1986.

The specialized lending and the wide geographic distribution of its commercial units, has made strict and effective lending controls at Fleet/Norstar Financial Group absolutely essential.

DECENTRALIZED LENDING, CENTRALIZED ADMINISTRATION

The commercial lending activities of Fleet/Norstar are administered by Charles W. Carey, executive vice president. He had the same responsibility with Fleet prior to the merger. Although the two banking companies are still in the process of bringing their operations together, there is now one credit policy for the entire organization. It is basically the Fleet policy developed under Carey's guidance.

MANAGING RISK

"We have tried to centralize the administrative aspects of the lending operation," Mr. Carey explained, "to be sure (among other things) that there is one place that knows where the risks are—a clearing house for risks, if you will."

One concern, as the financial organization has grown and expanded across state borders and is divided into several different banks—there are currently seven—has been to ensure that the company's exposure in any one area is controlled.

"We work hard at keeping our concentrations low," Carey said. "We have to be absolutely sure that we do not lend more than we want to a particular customer because the right hand doesn't know what the left hand is doing. This is easy to do when you get bigger." It is also easy to do when one company has divisions in different states or regions, perhaps even operating under different names. Fleet/Norstar reviews its loan exposure to a company and to an industry at the headquarters level to make sure it is below set limits.

Fleet/Norstar currently has a bankwide credit policy committee consisting of seven people, headed by Carey. Soon there will be a person in charge of loan policy at each of seven banks in the network. The senior credit policy committee, which does not pass on loans, does change policy when it is deemed necessary.

DECENTRALIZED LENDING

While centralizing the administration of the lending function, Fleet/Norstar decentralizes many of the credit decisions, as much as possible pushing things down to the local level.

As many banks do, Fleet/Norstar uses a loan rating system, and the loan officers making the loans also make the ratings. "We know loan officers will make some bad loans (hopefully not too many). But under our system, the worst thing a loan officer can do is misrate the loans," Carey told us.

There are seven ratings in the system:

1   (the best)

1A (close, but not the top)

2   (Good)

2B (OK)

3   (Subject to review)

4   (Doubtful)

5   (Lost)

Those comments are ours, based on remarks by Mr. Carey and other officials.

Loans are rarely put on the books if the rating is below 2; in certain circumstances, a 2B loan may be made, if it is watched very closely. Depending upon the size of the loan, the loan officer must discuss it with a senior loan officer. In addition, the officer must try to come up with work out programs with the borrowers when trouble develops. As Carey puts it, "As far as possible, the loan officers run the system."

Mr. Carey also states, "Our rating system is dynamic; the loan portfolio is updated daily. Actually," he added, "the system is more conservative than the measures used by the bank examiners. After all, we don't want them to tell us where our bad loans are; we ought to know them ourselves."

According to Carey, the loan department knows almost instantly when a loan deteriorates. "I get a weekly report on deteriorating ratings, and we get concerned when a loan moves from a '1' to a '2.' We don't want to see significant jumps in the ratings."

He reviews all "3" rated loans. When substantial discrepancies occur, he may meet the loan officer involved.

The system seems to be working, as Table 4–1, a summary of nonperforming assets as of March 31, 1988, and the other financial charts (Tables 4–2, 4–3, and 4–4) show.

TABLE 4–1
Nonperforming Assets

(thousands)	March 31, 1988	March 31, 1987	December 31, 1987
Nonperforming Assets:			
New England Banking	$ 52,588	$ 48,190	$ 34,994
New York Banking	54,951	29,587	48,164
Financial Services Subsidiaries	66,568	46,008	63,708
Lesser Developed Countries	854	28,472	862
Total	$174,961	$152,257	$147,728
Nonperforming assets as a percentage of outstanding loans and leases and other real estate owned (period-end)	1.04%	1.11%	.90%

TABLE 4–2
Financial Highlights, Fleet/Norstar Financial Group

| (thousands, except per share data) | Three Months Ended March 31 | | INCREASE |
	1988	1987	
Earnings			
Net Income	$ 75,488	$ 66,899	13%
Net interest income (fully taxable equivilant basis	269,730	251,295	7
Per Common Share			
Primary earnings	$ .75	$ .69	9%
Fully diluted earnings	.74	.68	9
Cash dividends declared	.2925	.21	39
Book Value	16.61	15.47	7
Operating Ratios			
Return on average assets	1.25%	1.24%	
Return on average common stockholders' equity	18.49	18.49	
Net interest margin	5.00	5.14	
Equity/assets ratio (period-end)	7.12	7.11	
At March 31			
Assets	$24,505,020	$22,165,787	11%
Stockholders' equity	1,744,392	1,576,402	11

Net Income Per Share (Fully diluted)	1stQ	2ndQ	3rdQ	4thQ	Year
1988	$.74				
1987	.68	$.42	$.69	$.01	$1.80
1986	.57	.59	.63	.65	2.44
1985	.47	.51	.51	.51	2.00

Prior year's earnings have been restated to reflect the retroactive implementation of Financial Accounting Standards Board Statement No. 91.

It should be pointed out that the rating system at Fleet/Norstar is not limited to actual loans. According to Mr. Carey, "We rate all our commitments. And we rate the banks we lend to."

He says that the Fleet/Norstar Financial Group concentrates on special industries, as noted in the lending summary at the beginning of this chapter. "We do not call on companies generally," he said, "but are driven by industries. As a result, we don't have general lending officers, but lending specialists." Unfortunately, he notes, even within the bank's specialities, there is more competition.

This places greater attention on the bank's lending officer training program.

LOAN OFFICER TRAINING

The training of loan officers at Fleet/Norstar, which is based on the program developed at Fleet, is one of the most extensive in the business. It is designed to provide trainees with the foundation necessary to assume account responsibilities in a lending division of the corporation. The program combines on-

TABLE 4–3
Net Chargeoffs

Years Ended December 31 (thousands)	1987	1986	1985
Consumer Loans	$ 33,237	$24,880	$14,252
Domestic Commercial Loans	13,602	13,074	19,711
International Commercial Loans	44,880	6.648	2,450
Leases	5.221	2,474	1,308
Real Estate Loans	6,905	713	633
Total	$103,845	$47,789	$38,354

Years Ended December 31 (thousands)	Net Chargeoffs as a Percentage of Average Loans and Leases		
	1987	1986	1985
Commercial Loans	.81%	.77%	.54%
Domestic Commercial Loans	.23	.26	.48
International Commercial Loans	23.01	2.69	.83
Leases	.74	.44	.29
Real Estate Loans	.19	.03	.03
Total	.72%	.41%	.41%

TABLE 4–4
Credit Loss Data, 1985–1987

	New England Banking	New York Banking	Non-Banking Subsidiaries	Subtotal	Latin American Loans	Total
Net chargeoffs as a percentage of average loans and leases:						
1987	.30%	.38%	.92%	.43%	34.27%	.72%
1986	.30	.26	.90	.37	3.66	.41
1985	.33	.22	1.09	.40	.66	.41
Reserves for losses as a percentage of year-end loans and leases:						
1987	1.18%	1.19%	1.96%	1.31%	100.00%	1.77%
1986	1.09	1.30	2.00	1.32	12.81	1.44
1985	.96	1.31	1.86	1.25	11.80	1.40
Coverage of net chargeoffs by year-end reserves for losses:						
1987	4.24×	3.64×	2.60×	3.47×	1.81×	2.79×
1986	4.22	5.63	2.54	4.02	3.30	3.94
1985	3.22	6.57	2.02	3.51	17.05	3.88

the-job training, course work, case studies, seminars, special assignments, and internships in various areas of the corporation in order to prepare candidates for lending assignments.

The program is divided into three phases, with progress into the next phase dependent upon the satisfactory completion of the stated requirements of the preceding phase. Depending upon academic and professional background, as well as motivation and learning capacity, the *average* stay in the program for BAs with no work experience will range from 15–18 months.

Some idea of the scope of the training program can be seen from this statement excerpted from material given to trainees:

> You will begin the program by participating in an intensive accounting course, followed by a seminar in analytical techniques. Other coursework includes Money and Banking and Finance. Upon successful completion of this education phase, you will begin to write analytical reports detailing the overall financial condition of existing customers and assessing risks. Working closely with management of the Credit Department as well as lending officers, you will begin to develop the knowledge required to make lending decisions as well as to increase your verbal communications skills.

Throughout the program, progress of the trainees is monitored by credit department management who are responsible for all facets of development, including work assignments and performance evaluations. Trainees receive regular feedback on performance and professional development. In addition to informal feedback received on exams and individual credit analyses, formal reviews are scheduled for each trainee on a quarterly basis. Furthermore, each candidate is assigned a mentor from the lending staff who serves as an informal advisor.

FLEET/NORSTAR MORTGAGE LENDING— A MAJOR BUSINESS

According to John W. Flynn, executive vice president and chief financial officer, the new organization's primary goal in this area is to be one of the five largest mortgage bankers in the country.

Last year (1987) was particularly good for Fleet/Norstar, according to Mr. Flynn, particularly when considering the difficulties of some banks. "I receive calls almost daily asking me to discuss or refute the thesis that mortgage banking is an exceptionally risky and volatile business. We just don't see it that way."

The mortgage banking risks that exist are the following:

Expense Risk
—Foreclosure
—Amortization
—General Overhead
Interest Rate Risk
—Inventory
—Pipeline
Principal Risk
—VA No-Bid

"In terms of expense, we, as the servicer, are responsible for foreclosing on delinquent mortgages and incurring the expenses that are involved in that foreclosure. I think it is false to say that with the refinancing of higher-rate mortgages that occurred last year, that risk is less today than it was twelve months ago. As the higher-rate mortgages have been paid off, the risk of foreclosure has been reduced," Flynn says. He continues:

> There are certain areas of the country—primarily in the oil belt—where foreclosures have been the highest; Fleet does not have a significant level of our servicing in those particular regions.
>
> In terms of amortization of purchased servicing—and we have been a big buyer of servicing—the accounting rules require that each quarter you go back and see if you are amortizing fast enough, based on your current experience rather than your anticipated experience when you made the purchase. The accounting rules require that if, in fact, you are amortizing too slowly, you have to catch up in the current quarter.
>
> There were thrifts in California last year which were required to book $50 million and $60 million special charges to get themselves in line. We have not had that problem because we think we've been very conservative in terms of original amortization.

As rates have gone higher, one of the plusses will be that our refinancings will slow down, and this risk will be even less going forward.

Finally, in terms of general overhead, Mr. Flynn says,

This is a business where the servicing fees are basically fixed. The people who are going to make the real money in this business are the lowest-cost producers, and based on the Mortgage Bankers of America's statistics, we have been one of the lowest-cost producers in this business for a long period of time.

In terms of interest rate risk, "we basically look at it in two pieces," he points out. "In terms of loans that we have actually closed and will be holding to put together into packages over the next thirty to ninety days, we have always hedged 100 percent of these loans. Usually, almost exclusively, we've done that through the use of forward commitments as opposed to options and futures.

"In terms of the pipeline," he notes, "which are the applications which are in various stages of process, we hedge anywhere from 40 percent to 90 percent. We would never hedge 100 percent because some applications are going to fall by the wayside. The customers change their mind, or they can't get the proper paperwork, or they go somewhere else. We normally average 75 percent, but after the events of April when rates erupted, we very quickly were in excess of 90 percent."

WHO IS FLEET/NORSTAR?

On March 18, 1987, Fleet Financial Group and Norstar Bancorp announced plans to merge. Completed on January 1, 1988, the merger created Fleet/Norstar Financial Group, Inc., a $25-billion diversified financial services company.

Based on assets, Fleet/Norstar is the nation's 22nd largest banking company. More importantly, it is the ninth largest institution in the country in terms of current market capitalization.

With nearly 1,000 offices in 39 states and two foreign locations, Fleet/Norstar employs approximately 18,750 people and maintains dual headquarters in Albany, N.Y., and Providence, R.I. The corporation's seven subsidiary banks are located in the Northeast; its nonbanking businesses operate from offices nationwide.

Lines of business include commercial and consumer banking, trust banking, mortgage banking and real estate lending, asset-based lending, consumer finance, student loan processing, and investment banking.

The completion of the merger united Fleet's and Norstar's banking affiliates in Maine to create Maine's largest bank. Bangor-based Merrill Bankshares, parent of Merrill Trust, and Portland-based Norstar Bank of Maine, merged to become Merrill/Norstar Bank.

Fleet/Norstar is one of the nation's top three mortgage banking companies. Fleet Mortgage and Fleet Real Estate Funding have 101 offices in 37 states. At year-end, Fleet/Norstar's mortgage servicing portfolio exceeded $27.7 billion.

The Corporation's brokerage subsidiary, Norstar Brokerage, is the nation's largest bank-owned discount brokerage firm with 22 offices in 14 states.

In 1987, Fleet Credit acquired Westinghouse Credit's leasing services division and Bankers Trust Company's equipment finance group. Fleet Credit now ranks among the 10 largest bank-owned leasing companies in the country and is the nation's largest small-ticket lessor.

The organization is progressing well, as Tables 4–1 through 4–4 clearly show. This progress is built upon a system of controls of its lending function that is one of the best in the industry.

CONTROL OF LENDING

Some of the biggest banking failures and near failures have occurred because the banks' lending activities were allowed to get out of control. Bad loans were made that shouldn't have been made in the first place; good (or reasonably good) loans were allowed to deteriorate to the point where they could not be salvaged; loan officers were not only encouraged but sometimes driven to produce while loan quality suffered; reviews of loans were perfunctory if there were reviews at all; and credit policy was ignored in the rush to bring in new business.

The horror stories go on. Too great a concentration of loans allowed to a single company, or to some specific industry, can—and has—spelled disaster. When a downturn hits that company or industry, the bank is left holding the loan paper—or some collateral it can do little or nothing with.

In many ways, bankers agree, the Penn Square debacle was a blessing in disguise for the banking industry. It caused many banks to look at their own shop and analyze more closely their loan policies and procedures, as well as their existing loan portfolios, and to institute controls.

A great number of banks tilted toward more conservative lending practices, a move that was probably overdue in certain instances. Unfortunately, some of the banks went too far, reducing risks to too low a minimum. This is foolish; it can hurt potential borrowers who could have become good customers, and it can do immeasurable harm to a bank that must compete in a dynamic market.

Still, it is safe to say that more loan policies have been committed to writing, and more monitoring procedures have been put in place during the past few years in the wake of Penn Square than at any time in our banking history. This is a positive development that should not have needed a disaster to come about.

Mining the Middle Market

In this chapter, it was noted that Fleet/Norstar concentrates its commercial lending on middle market companies. Several other banks profiled in this book are mining the same market. While this is a somewhat imprecise term, middle market generally refers to companies in the $10 million to $100 million sales range.

It is probably understandable that banks are going after this business. There are a considerable number of companies in this category, with more reaching this status every day. But another reason some banks have moved to the middle market is that they have had problems with lending to large firms.

Sometimes these companies have used their very size to force their banks to cater to their financial whims. They have sometimes caused a bank to tie up too large a proportion of its funds with them.

Then these large companies want additional money when demand is heavy, placing strains on the resources of the bank—but not using these resources when loan demand slows. Banks facing such dilemmas have sometimes said "enough," and have looked elsewhere for their business.

Keeping Loans under Control

A bank should certainly take steps to make sure bad loans don't get on its books. Fleet/Norstar does this to a considerable degree by placing the burden of proof on the lending officer who, of course, should best know his client. The officer rates his loans, and he'd better be accurate. This tempers any undue emphasis on building business too rapidly. This is particularly important when loan officers are paid incentives for new loans—as does Fleet/Norstar.

It is essential that new business be brought in, but it must be the right business.

As described earlier in this chapter, Fleet/Norstar does an admirable job of monitoring its loan portfolio. One of the all too frequent problems is that banks have been burned by bad loans that they didn't realize had turned sour. By continually rating a loan, the loan officer who made the loan must follow the progress of the borrower; if a problem develops, it can be (and usually is) caught before it is too late.

Even the best of borrowers can get into difficulty. So it is essential to work with that borrower and help it get out of trouble.

As banks have learned to their sorrow, the loan portfolio is too important not to be kept under control.

CHAPTER 5

THE EFFECTIVE USE OF TECHNOLOGY
First Wisconsin Is Making Milwaukee Known for Something Other Than Beer.

Change is one thing;
progress is another
—*Bertrand Russell*

Everyone knows that Milwaukee is famous for the brewing of beer. But as the site of sophisticated uses of technology in banking operations? Yet this is the case.

According to Walter Fiorentini, senior vice president and chief of the Information Services Division at First Wisconsin Corporation, this is not so surprising.

It seems that several years ago, Milwaukee was on its way to becoming a miniature money center. A lot of major companies located in the area, and First Wisconsin served many of the largest. In the 1960s, there was considerable exporting of manufactured goods from the Milwaukee area. This led to the bank developing extensive international banking facilities.

When dealing with these large firms, the bank had to handle substantial volumes of money transfers. First Wisconsin naturally went into the cash management. It was not long before the bank's range of services was equal to those of many money center banks.

As a consequence, it aggressively employed computers and other technological equipment.

We met with Walt Fiorentini and a number of his people to discuss how First Wisconsin moved from that point in the 1960s to its leadership position today as one of the more creative users of technology in banking. These people were Harvey Lippow, first vice president for development, Cindy Gear, and Kathleen Robbins, all with the Information Services Division, and Patricia Vander Grinten, vice-president in the Consumer Credit Division.

Ms. Vander Grinten noted that First Wisconsin was one of the original organizers of MasterCard. Because of its services to the manufacturing companies, the bank had a system in place.

She said that the bank began by purchasing a software package to handle charges. In the beginning, paper charges were transferred from the banks being served by mail. At the time, country club billing of charge slips was used, but the bank moved away from that system in 1974, one of the first banks to do so.

Actually, MasterCard was first developed in 1966. The bank provided cards to correspondents, using their names on the cards. Now, Walt Fiorentini notes, First Wisconsin services 600 correspondents who offer the cards to their customers. In a way, he said, they could be called "natural affinity" cards because of their relationship to First Wisconsin.

Technology was needed because market demand was building so fast. Therefore, it was either support the market or get out of it. Today over 25,000 merchants are signed up to accept cards processed by First Wisconsin.

Another push came in 1982, Ms. Vander Grinten said, when the MasterCard II debit card was announced. "We had to make sure we could handle the business when it came along."

"You start with the ability to manage the technology," Walt Fiorentini stated. "The user is always going to find new outlets, but if you have the ability to manage the technology, you will be able to serve the user."

Once you have had some success, Harvey Lippow said, "you can build on it. The track record here has been good," he adds, with understandable pride. "Another important factor is that at First Wisconsin, the user can communicate with the data processing people, which allows opportunities to be identified. Moreover, a variety of technologies have been intertwined."

Another advantage the bank enjoys, Kathleen Robbins noted, is its specialized method of matching orders to products. This makes the whole process easier.

Also, at First Wisconsin, Cindy Gear said, there is an open-mindedness about things. "If something doesn't work out, we discuss it."

This openness, Fiorentini added, has been developed on both sides—user and supplier. "After all, we have to work together," he said.

Also, Ms. Gear said, "We try to get people to explain 'why'."

"Organizations differ," Mr. Lippow said, even within much larger organizations. "Some are entrepreneurial and some are not. The charge card division here is entrepreneurial. As a result, people are willing to look beyond what is there. This team of ours," he added, "has more entrepreneurial fire than some others do."

Mr. Fiorentini agrees. "The credit card people here have a commitment to perform excellently. And when things don't work out they go on trying." After all, Ms. Gear went on, "Even simple projects don't always go perfectly."

RESEARCH AND DEVELOPMENT

Since the First Wisconsin network has grown so large, Patricia Vander Grinten observed, "we couldn't survive without state-of-the-art technology."

That is one of the reasons the company embarked on a $1.7 million project in the fall of 1985. It was intended to replace the card system then in effect with one easier to work with. Or, as Walt Fiorentini put it, "It was very much an investment in the future."

Actually, he pointed out, users were not complaining at that juncture. However, both the users and the technical people at First Wisconsin decided that the investment in a new and improved system would be worthwhile. Not only that, there were some changes that had to be made in the system, "so why not make some major changes while we're at it?" was the decision that prevailed.

In some ways, the decision to make a commitment for a substantial system change is typical of the approach at First Wisconsin. As Cindy Gear noted, "We work closely with customers to help solve their problems." This is an approach, Harvey Lippow pointed out, "that is not the case everywhere."

"We are willing to take some risks," Ms. Gear noted. And the project that began in 1985 was a considerable risk on First Wisconsin's part.

"If you don't take reasonable, controlled risks," Walt Fiorentini said, "you won't grow. Which means that you must have an environment in which risks are allowed to be taken."

The $1.7 million risk began to pay off for the bank in January of 1987 when the final phase of the project was installed.

EMBARKING ON NEW PROJECTS

First Wisconsin is now involved in a new $1.3 million project that is designed to give the bank's system greater flexibility, putting the organization in a competitive position for the next five years.

An important point was stressed by Mr. Fiorentini: the steering committee composed of the bank's senior management supported the plan as devised by the Information Services Division and gave it the green light.

The plan, Ms. Vander Grinten said, is one that can adjust to changes as they occur. This is also of great importance with change so prevalent in banking technology.

Reiterating a point made earlier, Harvey Lippow said that the company's users "have enough confidence in our technology group that the members can deal with (user) requirements. Our track record has helped to bolster this confidence."

"Well," Patricia Vander Grinten added, "we are not used to taking 'no' for an answer."

THE TRAINING FACTOR

Any product that goes out to First Wisconsin's banking customers, including the network of correspondents, includes extensive training materials and manuals. "In addition," Lippow said, "we also have ongoing programs to handle questions that users might have. We also go out and teach merchants on how to use our systems and help them change their procedures. A good part of our job is providing assistance."

On those manuals, Fiorentini said it was important to have the information properly laid out, "so considerable attention is paid to this aspect."

"We continually refine the training we do," Mr Lippow said. Where possible, "we use the technology itself to help users understand the system."

Walt Fiorentini noted that members of the technology group meet once a year with all the banks using the First Wisconsin system. There is an ongoing dialogue between users and the bank. "This fosters confidence and points up areas where more work is needed," he said.

RESEARCH AND NEW DEVELOPMENTS

Everyone in the technology group at First Wisconsin attempts to keep abreast with the latest developments. For example, Mr. Fiorentini said, they have been looking at so-called "expert" systems which are supposedly capable of making decisions. At this stage, the bank is not prepared to make any decisions of its own on such systems.

According to Harvey Lippow, the bank has a development center which looks into productivity and communications. "We have people who are knowledgeable about trends. However," he added pointedly, "we don't have a whole bunch of solutions looking for a problem."

He said that those in the technology group look at new products with this question in mind: "How can it help us?" Also, because they are working on a project that called for tools not available in-house, "we had to go outside and we had to know what was available there."

The objective, he added, "is to make sure that the user and the technology team is working on the same wave length. The tools being used are to help our users find what they want."

THE PEOPLE PRIORITY

First Wisconsin, along with other banks making good use of technology, is always on the lookout for good people, but those in this discussion said the quality of the people on board is high. Moreover, they point out that the turnover rate at First Wisconsin is lower than the national average.

"We spend a lot of time and money on 'people' problems," Lippow noted. When people are hired, they are put into a career plan.

Walt Fiorentini said that the people issue has never taken "second place in anything we have done."

MERGERS AND BANK SYSTEMS

During the past year or so, First Wisconsin has moved aggressively into the neighboring states of Illinois and Minnesota, adding new banks to its network. This has presented the problem of getting the different systems in use at those banks to work together.

But, as Harvey Lippow states, First Wisconsin has been doing just that for years. "We take for granted that we will be able to handle the processing needs of other banks; and when we do, this means an immediate payback. We will take over their processing and supply them with what they need." However, he adds, "this sometimes presents a major obstacle to getting people to feel they are part of the corporate system."

SYSTEMS AND SOFTWARE

Mr. Fiorentini stated that "when we develop a system, we want it to have a longer life than is generally the case."

Software is usually out-of-date in seven or eight years, Lippow noted. "But with the right design, its life can extend to twelve to fifteen years."

"We are working on a deposit system," he stated. "Actually we couldn't find what we wanted elsewhere, so we decided to build our own. When it is completed, and this is expected by the end of next year, 200 banks will be converted to the system.

"In our development work, we use all sorts of assistance; if necessary, we will go outside and use consultants. Our objective is to build a quality system with great flexibility."

The bank recently developed a system (with the assistance of IBM) to improve the teller functions. It is a system designed to run without a manual.

"While there is no manual," Mr. Fiorentini said, "the instructions are put up on the screen. With it, a teller doesn't have to ask for information already in the system. It will update information, issue forms, and when the buttons are pushed, an account is instantly opened. The result is a system that provides greater efficiency and that eliminates errors."

"Our systems do not meet the requirements of all our users," he commented, "so we are constantly updating them. Although," he added, "at this stage, we cannot afford to be all things to all users."

Mr. Fiorentini also mentioned costs, one thing that can destroy a system—and has, at many banks. "We do our best to be cost-effective. We have found the best way to measure data processing expense is use cost per adjusted transaction, which contains operating expenses and payment for new projects."

"At First Wisconsin, we have sensitive cost controls—and we try to run our systems as close to capacity as possible—currently, we are operating at between 90–95 percent of capacity."

He also said it helps to achieve high productivity. "The best way to achieve optimum productivity," he said, "Is to have things done right the first time."

That exalted level of performance may not always be achieved at First Wisconsin's Information Services Division and other units of the technology group. Still, they seem to be extremely close to it.

TECHNOLOGY IN PERSPECTIVE

First Wisconsin not only provides data processing services to its own units and member banks but to may other banks around the country. It has a successful track record in this area for a number of reasons, and not the least of these is that First Wisconsin started several years ago to find out what all the users of its data processing wanted and needed. This has continued to be a feature of the way it operates. It also is one that not enough other suppliers of services seem to understand.

Over the years this research has consistently resulted in three primary challenges:

1. To make better decisions, better information is required; not more information, because there's too much of that already, but more concise, clearer, more useful information.

2. To improve operational efficiency, easier-to-use technology is a must. Put another way, technology that improves productivity is useless if it's too complicated for people to understand and operate easily.

3. To stay ahead of the competition, flexible and sophisticated services and marketing support are essential. This support should help provide detailed information about a bank's market; enable a bank to develop products and services unique to its customer base; help communicate service offerings to customers quickly, easily and professionally; and help distinguish the bank from its competition by a high level of service quality.

ACCESS TO A DATA BASE

The user of automated services, among other things, wants information. First Wisconsin has come up with a program called ACCESS which, in effect, gives each user its own data base.

With the easy-to-use ACCESS, banks can quickly and easily retrieve current and historical information about their customers, manipulate it, synthesize it, analyze it whenever necessary, and come away with assistance in

- Strategic planning
- Market identification
- Product and pricing analyses
- Cross-sell opportunities
- Performance monitoring
- Mailing label generation

In effect banks can address heretofore hard-to-answer questions such as

• Cross-Sell Identification. How many of my households have more than $5,000 in balances and use three or more services?
• Pricing Impact Analysis. If we institute a charge for low-balance savings accounts, how many affluent households would be impacted?

ACCESS lets a bank ask virtually any question it wants to and provides results for interpretation, projection and exploration of almost any action plan or new product before taking it to market.

COPING WITH DISASTER

One of the features of a successful network system is its ability to deal with the unexpected.

Earlier this year a fire in Hinsdale, Illinois, shut down the phone lines there, including phones to banks in the area which was part of First Wisconsin's data processing service. Gerald Ried, the bank's director of operations, sales and services, explained the situation.

> This service outage affected a number of our Illinois users. No online processing was available at all. And, of course, they couldn't contact us.
>
> After confirmation with Illinois Bell, we immediately put together a disaster recovery program.
>
> Within one day, a team of various specialists developed an alternative routing plan for each impacted bank to re-establish full data communications. The following day appropriate equipment was personally delivered and installed by our technicians so that banks could resume normal activity processing.

STATE OF THE ART IN WISCONSIN

Any bank that wants to make its mark in the use of technology must utilize the latest advances in equipment. Here are some examples of what First Wisconsin is using and how the equipment is applied:

• Through an advanced diagnostics system, potential problems in any of First Wisconsin's high-speed data transmission lines can be quickly identified, located and remedied, thus keeping downtime to a minimum. If something goes wrong, employees work with a video terminal to determine quickly and accurately the nature, location, and scope of the problem.

• First Wisconsin's Information Services Division uses high capacity fiber optics technology, strands of glass each thinner than a human hair, for exceptionally cost-effective transmission of voice and data. Beams of message-carrying light travel through the fiber optic strands at incredible rates of speed.

• Maintaining a library of computer data, which used to involve large, space-consuming reels, is now done more easily and efficiently with compact tapes. The processor and tapes offer the added advantage of much greater reliability.

First Wisconsin's strong position in check collection is largely the result of its ability to offer better service at lower cost. While the equipment and some of the software used are the same as at other banks, its programmers have developed systems capable of handling double the current work load of almost 1.5 million checks a day. This unusually large capacity is one reason for the popularity of "Control Disbursement," a cash management service. Customers are provided final check clearing information before the start of the business day. This enables them to maximize cash flow by making fiscal decisions daily. Excess cash can be invested; if borrowing is required, it can be limited to the amount needed to fund presented checks.

The computer has become the "factory" of the financial industry, churning out products and services that have revolutionized personal and corporate financial management. It has expanded the array of banking services for commercial customers and virtually dictates a bank's consumer products— products which have been accounting for an expanding share of the banking industry's profits. The computer is also the tool that is enabling some banks' managements to improve profitability through sounder planning and cost control.

This has certainly been the case at First Wisconsin.

MAKING TECHNOLOGY WORK FOR
YOUR BANK

First Wisconsin is making it work for the Milwaukee-based banking company. But it is also obvious from the preceding information that the people at the bank work at making it work.

The technology personnel at First Wisconsin are confident, capable—and pragmatic. They do not expect technology to do it all, although in certain areas, they believe they have the capacity to accomplish a great deal.

Confident. Capable. Pragmatic. Those are three features that an electronic banking company will find invaluable, and that will help make it be more successful.

The people we met with strongly stated the need to work closely with the users of the system—inside and outside the bank. Be ready to be of service; try to work out problems together with users; keep current with developments; and try to keep costs under control.

These are things that are not always easy to do. Yet they may well be the essential ingredients if technology is to be managed and managed creatively.

One thing that First Wisconsin does *not* do, that other banks sometimes do, is to package their systems for sale to other banks.

By doing this, of course, the bank could reduce costs, perhaps significantly. But this is not the route First Wisconsin is traveling. Moreover, they indicate that the bank has no plans at present to change routes.

On the other hand, one thing First Wisconsin does extremely well is allow risk taking. Just as lenders can completely fulfill their obligations to their bank or to the market only by taking risks and making some bad loans, the data processing area or function of a bank must also be willing to take some risks—but only for those who have studied the plans with care.

CHAPTER 6

CONTROLLING DECENTRALIZED OPERATIONS STATEWIDE
Barnett Banks Is Building Its Florida Franchise with an Entrepreneurial Style

> Bankers are not as
> stupid as they look.
> —*SEC Investigation of Gulf & Western,*
> *New York Times*

Barnett Banks of Florida may have one of the best banking organizations in the country. Most assuredly, it has a strong management team at the headquarters office in Jacksonville. Perhaps this explains why its decentralized organization, which covers almost all of Florida worth covering, is doing so well.

A free-wheeling discussion of management issues was held earlier this year with a six-member group consisting of

Charles E. Rice, 53, chairman, president and chief executive officer.

Albert D. Ernest, Jr., 58, vice chairman, responsible for larger banking units.

Earl B. Hadlow, 62, vice chairman and general counsel.

Thomas H. Jacobsen, 49, vice chairman, responsible for corporate lending.

Allen L. Lastinger, Jr., 46, vice chairman, responsible for community banks and consumer lending.

Stephen A. Hansel, 41, senior executive vice president and chief financial officer.

The meeting was held in a conference room just outside Mr. Rice's office.

RICE:

> Barnett [which consists of 33 banking and 11 nonbanking affiliates] is not a loose confederation. Each operates under its own budget. Bank presidents are held accountable for their units and rewarded accordingly. All of them can receive bonuses of as much as 50 percent of their base salaries—even if they are located in a slow market. This bonus system, which extends down to the level of vice president, first began in 1972.

ERNEST:

> All our units have common goals, objectives, and policies. We are a shareholder driven, financially driven, market driven organization. We try to balance growth and profitability. This lends itself to a decentralized setup.

LASTINGER:

> Barnett operates in a very diversified market. Marketing plans are tailored to the specific area.

ERNEST:

> We operate in an autonomous style, right to the branch level.

JACOBSEN:

> Every year we try to outgrow the market; 250 branches have been built over the past 11 years.

RICE:

> Almost all the management growth at Barnett has been internal. We hire about 300 college graduates every year. In their training, they are given multiple career paths to a limited extent which they may follow.

Operational Structure

RICE:

> Each profit center has its own capital base, and each one is performance driven. Our multi-bank structure is historic since that was all we were allowed to have in Florida. In the acquisitions

of banks over the years, we have had a pretty good success rate in making the people at those banks Barnett people. Of course, we have never had what could be described as a mega-merger. Actually, with our strategies, it would be difficult to acquire a really big bank.

ERNEST:

Our way of running a business is entrepreneurial. People like to run their own business.

JACOBSEN:

Moreover, our people are paid well.

HANSEL:

We often have problems finding all the people, and the right kind of people, we need because we have been growing so fast.

ERNEST:

At the headquarters office, we try to be supportive of our presidents and their people.

LASTINGER:

I believe we have a reputation of being fair with people. Another element that helps us gain the allegiance of people coming into the organization is that the organization continues to grow.

In addition, each of our units has its own lending limits.

HANSEL:

With many centralized operations, loan authority is the first thing to go, to be taken away.

ERNEST:

We try to keep the decision making close to the market. Customers like this: they don't have to wait for decisions to come down from the head office.

RICE:

After an acquisition takes place, the operation of the unit remains essentially the same. Local boards of directors stay in place. However, the board cannot come between the president of the bank and Barnett headquarters.

HANSEL:

> One of our strong points is that we have an open reporting system. Everybody is able to look at everybody else's numbers. This is an ongoing thing, so that people always know what others are doing. And peer pressure works.

RICE:

> The proof is in the performance. Last year, 1987, we had a 100 percent year because our profit goals were met.

JACOBSEN:

> There is also flexibility, with room to move within a range.

RICE:

> Barnett can be described as "reactive" because we respond to the needs of the marketplace.

JACOBSEN:

> One of the reasons we can respond is because we have a number one position in many functional areas.

Planning

RICE:

> The planning process is important at Barnett. Many of our plans are generated in the field and contribute to overall corporate plans.

ERNEST:

> Each of our individual banks has a strategic plan. Barnett imposes the concept of planning on a bank if it did not have a planning process before joining us. Planning allows us to design and engineer performance results.

JACOBSEN:

> Whether it is lending or some other activity, it is important to have things done at the local level.

HANSEL:

> At the same time, it is important that the systems work in sync.

JACOBSEN:

We are in business to take credit risks, but not market risks.

HANSEL:

What we are really trying to do is focus on earnings share. We want to build a good franchise.

The above excerpts from the discussion indicate a number of things about how Barnett is run. First, although Charlie Rice is obviously in charge, he does not try to dominate a meeting. In a normal workday, there are often many informal meetings where some or all members of this senior group exchange ideas, solicit comments, and argue points. Rice, who has been chief executive since 1979, selected the team members, and he encourages them to interact on all matters of concern to the banking company.

The meeting also demonstrates the commitment Barnett Banks has to the concept of decentralization and the encouragement of entrepreneurism throughout the organization.

PROGRESS THROUGH DECENTRALIZATION

One of Barnett's strengths is that it tries to keep decisions as close as possible to its customers. It aggressively pursues the available market by encouraging each bank to develop local programs and implement local ideas through its extensive office network. This gives it an advantage, especially against more centralized competitors.

In its decentralized structure, each of Barnett's 33 affiliate banks has a president, management team, and local board of directors. Each bank serves a different market, and in each Barnett has deep community roots.

Each bank is responsible for policy decisions affecting its customers. Barnett believes the people who work in a market should shape the strategies because they know best what their customers need and expect. This allows the company to keep a personal touch despite its overall size.

These bank presidents and 500 office managers are given the authority and responsibility to run their own businesses.

Each must accept responsibility for the bottom line. This sense of ownership sets Barnett apart from its peers.

This does not mean that control is not exercised. It is. Every month a "performance ranking" is issued.

The report is sent to an extensive list of management people including, of course, the president of the individual banks. The ranking is based on market share; growth in such areas as deposits, loans, and earnings; loan losses; and the cost of gathering deposits.

Individual bank performance is compared with goals that have previously been set, with year-earlier results, and with the performance of the other banks.

Banks at or near the bottom of the list are targeted for special attention, including visits from people from the home office. It is also well understood that a bank better not stay around the bottom of the ranking for very long. If it does, it is very likely some management changes will be made.

Still, with all this pressure to perform, morale seems to be high. But this is understandable because, in spite of the close monitoring, rewards are high, and there is the autonomy. As one of the individual bank presidents said in an article on Barnett in *The Wall Street Journal* several months ago, being in charge of a Barnett Bank "isn't a lot different from running an independent bank."

MARKET SHARE GROWTH

For the past few years Barnett has been on a roll. It continues to capture a greater share of Florida's banking deposits than any other single banking organization or group of banks. By December 31, 1987, the bank's share of individual, partnership, and corporate deposits in Florida increased to 22.41 percent— more than 1,000 share points above the nearest competitor. The increase in market share reflects more than $1 billion in internal growth and was achieved as all other major competitors lost market share or remained relatively flat.

Barnett's deposit-growth success is due in large part to its extensive office network. By the end of the first quarter of 1988, they offered the convenience of 498 offices in Florida. Together with 14 offices in Georgia, Barnett's total distribution network consists of 512 offices and 493 automated teller machines. (See Figure 6–1.)

GROWTH AND PROFITS

Perhaps Barnett's greatest achievement has been its success in balancing financial performance with substantial growth.

FIGURE 6–1
Barnett's Franchise

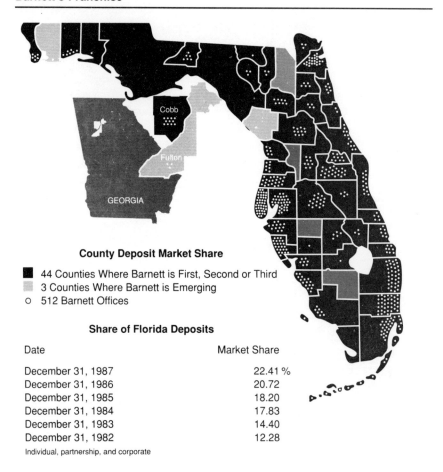

County Deposit Market Share

■ 44 Counties Where Barnett is First, Second or Third
▨ 3 Counties Where Barnett is Emerging
○ 512 Barnett Offices

Share of Florida Deposits

Date	Market Share
December 31, 1987	22.41 %
December 31, 1986	20.72
December 31, 1985	18.20
December 31, 1984	17.83
December 31, 1983	14.40
December 31, 1982	12.28

Individual, partnership, and corporate

Twelve years ago, as the bank emerged from Florida's last major recession, it was a $2-billion-asset company. Since then it has expanded more than tenfold and now has assets of $23 billion.

Most of this has been achieved since 1977 when branch banking was permitted in Florida. The bank has built 239 new offices at a cost of $130 million, which together have attracted deposits of more than $5.5 billion. In 1987 they earned $51 million for a return on an investment of 39 percent.

This construction program has been supplemented by strategic acquisitions. In the last two years alone Barnett has, through the assimilation of three major organizations, added $3.5 billion in assets that position it as a market leader in those areas. This was done at a cost of approximately $372 million or about 12 cents per dollar of deposits.

Management believes a cost-effective acquisition program to achieve market entry or to build market power is the right strategy, in contrast to acquiring for the sake of size alone. Thus, market strength has been achieved without sacrificing earnings targets in any year.

New office sites are carefully located to assure an early return on investment. Acquisitions are reviewed from many perspectives and priced to minimize earnings dilution.

AND MARKET LEADERSHIP

Today Barnett is a market leader in 44 of the 46 counties it serves. There is a Barnett office within a few minutes of 9 out of 10 Floridians, and the company serves one of Georgia's fastest-growing major counties. No other bank comes this close to market coverage.

With the advent of interstate activity, many out-of-state banks have tried to gain similar strength in Florida by acquiring existing institutions in the state. Since 1980, all but three of the 15 Florida-based major bank holding companies have disappeared.

Further, the entry to Florida by these out-of-state superregional banks has created turmoil in the marketplace, resulting in deposit share losses for their new acquisitions. In fact, of all the major banks now in Florida, only Barnett continues to gain significant market share.

Its strategy has been to concentrate on critical markets and growth markets rather than on size of interstate expansion for its own sake. Out-of-state opportunities are carefully assessed under a policy adopted three years ago to focus primarily on Florida and secondarily on other southeastern states. Florida has deposit growth of more than 10 percent, unmatched by any of the others. In fact, 15 of the 22 southeastern metropolitan areas with deposits of more than $500 million and a deposit growth rate of 10 percent or more are in Florida.

That's why Barnett has concentrated on Florida, but it's also why the bank's entry into Atlanta in 1987 was predictable. Cobb County, the third largest in Georgia, is one of the fastest growing counties in the United States. The agreement to acquire First Fulton Bank & Trust allows Barnett to expand further throughout Greater Atlanta.

THE BARNETT FRANCHISE

Barnett Banks has many things going for it, but two of the most important are the state of Florida and its excellent management team. As Prudential-Bache stock analyst George Salem says, "Super management, super region."

Fabulous Florida

The economy of Florida and its bright prospects are discussed in some detail in Chapter 2. These prospects mean that other banks are counting on capitalizing on the Sunshine State.

But, certainly, Barnett looks at the market in a somewhat different way. "Montgomery Securities notes that Barnett's style and preference is first to let the strong growth of Florida influence the revenue line. Then they purge loan losses and follow up by closely managing expenses as the safety valve in order to achieve numbers that they desire."

"Barnett has put into place a structure of offices that

reminds us of a very successful retail chain," Montgomery Securities states. "Over half of their offices are less than 10 years old, meaning that one can look forward to profit additions from maturing stores. In addition, if Barnett were ever to need earnings, all they would have to do is slow down the branch expansion slightly and they could achieve their ends. Barring the need to do that, however, the company can continue to put intense pressure on its competitors by expanding its already huge presence in and around the state, penetrating each particular county more deeply."

When announcing Barnett's strong performance earlier this year, (see Table 6–1), Charles Rice said, "Our strategy has been to harness Florida's natural growth, balance it with strong profitability, and thereby achieve strong and consistent earnings increases for our shareholders while at the same time building our franchise."

EMPHASIS ON THE ENTREPRENEURIAL

Perhaps the single key factor that explains how Barnett is able to control effectively its decentralized operations throughout Florida (and one county in Georgia) is its nurturing of the entrepreneurial spirit.

In a lecture at the University of Miami, Barnett's chief executive Charles Rice discussed his concept of entrepreneurship and what his organization does to foster it, as these excerpts illustrate:

> I'm here to propose that there is life after the small business and that the entrepreneurial spirit lives on. It is not the exclusive domain of small business. . . .

> By standard definitions, Barnett is not small. And yet, I believe quite firmly that we have retained—in fact, we have nurtured—the entrepreneurial spirit. This, then, is my thesis today . . . that the entrepreneurial spirit can survive and thrive in a large organization.

> The key to this, in a word, is for the large organization to religiously behave like a small one and for its management to be committed to this rather simple philosophy. . . .

TABLE 6-1
Financial Highlights

For the Three Months Ended March 31—Dollars in Thousands Except Per Share Data	1988	1987	Change
For the Period			
Net interest income (taxable equivalent)	$253,474	$236,400	7%
Provision for loan losses	20,746	23,661	(12)
Non-interest income	79,570	66,524	20
Non-interest expense	228,127	200,029	14
Net income	53,591	46,166	16
Per Share			
Primary earnings	$ .89	$ .78	14%
Fully diluted earnings	.89	.77	16
Cash dividends declared	.23	.20	15
Common book value	22.28	19.82	12
Common stock price:			
High	35.88	39.00	(8)
Low	29.00	31.38	(8)
Close	32.75	36.88	(11)
Key Performance Ratios			
Return on average assets	.92%	.87%	6%
Return on average shareholders' equity	16.29	15.98	2
Taxable-equivalent net yield on average earning assets	4.81	4.96	(3)
Overhead ratio	68.50	66.03	4
Ratio of shareholders' equity to total assets at period end	5.59	5.47	2
Primary Capital to total assets at period end	7.81	7.82	—
Dividend payout ratio	25.78	24.82	4
At Period End			
Assets	$23,823,362	$21,481,541	11%
Deposits	20,667,958	18,930,306	9
Loans, net of unearned income	17,524,128	15,253,152	15
Earning assets	21,412,603	19,180,407	12
Shareholders' equity	1,332,039	1,174,421	13
Common shares outstanding	59,680,904	58,698,904	2
Average Balances			
Assets	$23,400,267	$21,252,430	10%
Deposits	20,293,034	18,526,548	10
Loans, net of unearned income	17,228,143	14,985,862	15
Earning assets	21,073,739	19,069,335	11
Shareholders' equity	1,315,891	1,155,578	14
Common equivalant shares outstanding	60,464,094	59,192,378	2
Fully diluted shares outstanding	60,464,094	60,032,069	1

Restated to reflect the combination of Barnett and Home Federal Bank of Florida, F.S.B. and the adoption of SFAS No. 91.

The key is to cultivate and foster such a spirit in the organization. How is this done?

The main objectives are few: keep the operation simple. The more complex it becomes, the more it resembles a bureaucracy, and we all know that there's nothing endearing about that.

Secondly, while the universal goal is results, the results must be measurable. The company must be able to see improvement, and each employee must be able to recognize his or her contributions.

Finally, performance must be consistent over time. It's not good enough to give a 100 percent effort one year and fall back to 50 percent a year later. The effort and the performance must be fine-tuned and even. . . .

Each bank is responsible for policy decisions affecting its local market. We believe the people who have to work by the rules should have a hand in making the rules. What may be a good business decision in Jacksonville may not be the best decision in Miami or Orlando. . . .

Now, on the other side of the coin, each of our presidents is responsible for the profitable performance of that bank. In terms of gaining deposits, making quality loans, protecting margins or improving market share, it is the bank president who is accountable for the bottom line. There are monthly comparisons of every criteria imaginable between profit centers within Barnett, and quarterly peer group comparisons within the industry.

Each of our presidents and branch office managers has the authority and the responsibility to do the best job possible. They are absolutely accountable with the same risk/reward consequences as any other entrepreneur. . . .

Carrying this premise a step further, let me describe how we compensate our bank presidents. Their salaries and bonuses are based on the performance of their bank, and each bank has different objectives. This emphasis provides incentive to succeed and not merely to "get by." So, with this incentive to succeed in place, the steps necessary to achieve success lie squarely with the president. . . .

Of equal importance is that these goals are communicated through the ranks. It's essential that everyone on the team understand, subscribe to and support the objectives of the company.

The most effective way to do this is for each employee, from the mail clerk to the president to think, feel, and behave like an owner.

To do that you've got to give them opportunities and incentives to become owners, through stock purchase plans, stock options, and other means. The result can be a company of entrepreneurs, each willing to assume the risks of managing their responsibilities to achieve the overall goals of the entire organization. . . .

We believe Barnett is able to provide—through our management structure, compensation and benefit plans and general philosophy—the elements sought by those individuals who turn to self-employment. We practice entrepreneurial management. . . .

DECENTRALIZATION UNDER CONTROL

Barnett Banks runs a statewide franchise very smoothly, almost unobtrusively.

In some ways, the managerial control exercised is difficult to see. It's there, for sure, but it usually does not cause many ripples unless, of course, a local bank, operating rather autonomously, gets into trouble or decides to run things in a manner that is not considered "the Barnett way." Then it would readily become apparent who calls the shots.

The Barnett way perhaps can be described as controlled decentralization. The 34 separate bank presidents are quite independent, reporting to vice chairmen of the holding company who, in turn, report to the chairman.

Of course, there are guidelines that must be followed, and products are uniform in the 500 plus banking offices. Bankwide (and statewide) plans are formulated at the holding company and then communicated to the banking companies. Goals are set after consultations with the individual banks—and those goals are expected to be met. If they are not met, there had better be compelling reasons for the failure of performance.

As noted above, the 34 banking affiliates receive a detailed report every month that provides pertinent operating data. This shows that each bank is being closely monitored, not only in the Jacksonville headquarters, but by all the other banks in the system. Peer pressure not only exists, it works.

The thing is, the Barnett Banks do operate independently. They make loans (within guidelines) at the bank and even at the branch level. This counters some of the problems often voiced by customers of large banks, who complain of endless red tape and the fact that "None of the bankers I deal with can make a decision; everything must be pushed up to the main office while I wait."

This can be a frustrating situation and it has, at times, opened the door to new banks designed to perform special services (see "Finding a Niche," Chapter 10).

The "Barnett way" won't work for every banking company that operates areawide or statewide or regionwide. It calls for a special culture that probably is nurtured over several years. For many banks, more control, more hands-on-control, if you will, is more appropriate and more workable for them.

But for others, Barnett's use of independence and its encouragement of entrepreneurism is an alternative with many positive features, including these:

• Headquarters staff can be relatively lean (and doesn't often have to be mean). For instance, there are less than 400 people employed in Barnett's holding company, and almost no middle managers.

• Local banks that are part of the system can enjoy the best of both worlds—community banks with big bank clout.

For banks that are primarily retail-oriented, as is Barnett, decentralization allows them to mine the local markets as no big bank can. With effective controls in place, the bottom line can be most impressive.

PART 3

DEVELOPING BUSINESS

Perhaps the essence of banking growth and progress can be reduced to two simple words: *business development.*

Over the years, banking institutions have always been concerned with adding new business. But for a good part of the history of banking, the business was brought in through what can charitably be described as haphazard methods. Most of it was accomplished through friends, relatives, business associates, and because the bank just happened to "be there."

After World War II, banking, at least in the money centers, became more business-like. Borrowing from the techniques developed for manufacturing concerns, financial institutions started to actively, effectively, systematically go after new customers. Still, the idea that "sales" or "marketing" were important elements in the business of banking was not part of most bankers' mind sets.

It really has only been with the advent of deregulation during the past decade that banking institutions have finally gotten down to the nitty-gritty of increasing business, adding customers, doing market research, putting some creativity into advertising, developing new products and services.

Banking today is not like banking was just a generation ago. Technological advances, of course, have brought banking into the electronic age. And competition—from other banks, from thrift institutions, and from a host of nonbank financial organizations—has brought banking into an era of business development.

Sales is now a word and a concept that is finally being accepted (though sometimes grudgingly) by most banking companies. Advertising—aggressive, innovative, clever—is now essential to bank growth. And marketing specialists are even being promoted to the top echelons of a growing number of banks.

In addition, increased attention is being given to good customer relations and there is a growing awareness that banking is truly a service business—with emphasis on service. And it's about time. With more competition coming into the financial marketplace daily, customers—corporate and individual—are more sophisticated today. They can no longer be taken for granted. Any bank that is doing its job effectively in 1988 knows that and acts upon that knowledge.

At the same time that more attention is being given to bank marketing activities, the basics of prudent banking must not be slighted. In fact, with pressures to add loans and build fee income, it is vital that financial principles be strictly followed. After all, Penn Square was only six short years ago.

But here we are, with business development now an essential ingredient in the mix of banking functions. It has almost become an art form, as the three examples that follow illustrate so well.

CHAPTER 7

MAKING MONEY IN
A DEPRESSED ECONOMY
How Hibernia Corporation
has done it.

Waiting for supply side
economics to work is like
leaving the landing lights
on for Amelia Earhart.
—*Walter Heller*

The last few years have not been good ones for Louisiana. Much of the wealth in the Bayou State is related to energy, both oil and gas. Prices, particularly oil prices, dropped precipitously in the early and mid-1980s; for businesses depending on oil, the times could charitably be described as a disaster.

New Orleans, the queen city of the Mississippi, has had several rough years, bottoming out in 1984–85 just when the Louisiana World Exposition was expected to brighten the economic picture and put new life into New Orleans and its environs. The fair did little but underscore the low level of the economy. For that matter, even the New Orleans Saints football team was hardly a draw; the team had made a habit of losing. And when people did come to a game, they found that the Superdome roof leaked.

The seriousness of the economy in Louisiana cannot be overstated, although the picture has been brightening during the past year. After peaking at close to 15 percent in January of 1986, the unemployment rate dropped to under 10 percent by mid-1988. The price of oil has risen well above its 1986 lows and oil-related activity has increased. One indication of this is that the number of oil rigs operating in the state increased by 44 percent during 1987.

Tourism in New Orleans is again on the rise with a number of new hotels being built. This past summer saw the Republican National Convention boost the local economy. The Saints actually made the playoffs earlier in the year—and the roof of the Superdome is being resurfaced.

That's not to say that all is well. The state's rate of unemployment is still the second highest in the country. The price of oil remains relatively low. At the beginning of the decade, when the oil boom was still on, Louisiana ranked thirty-first in per capita income; currently it ranks forty-sixth. The economy is still in the doldrums.

Along with many other industries in Louisiana, banking has suffered in the post–oil boom economy. But one banking company has been able to weather the economic storms and even posted consistent gains during the state's economic downturn—Hibernia Corporation.

HOW HIBERNIA HAS DONE IT

The performance of Hibernia Corporation and the Hibernia National Bank over the past few years has been sparkling. Now the largest bank holding company in Louisiana, it has assets of over $5 billion and has set new records of growth each year in assets, earnings per share, deposits, loans, and shareholders' equity.

There are four major banking organizations in the state. In addition to Hibernia, these are First National Bank of Commerce, Louisiana National Bank, and Whitney National Bank. Figures 7–1a and 7–1b compare the performance of these four in two important areas, loans and deposits. Quite obviously, Hibernia has outdistanced its competition.

Another picture of how Hibernia has done is provided by Figures 7–2 and 7–3 which compare major banking companies in the "oil patch" states of Louisiana, Oklahoma, and Texas in 1986—near the low point for energy-based economies—in two important measures of performance, return on assets and return on equity. Again, Hibernia did remarkably well.

Throughout the economic downturn, and continuing into

FIGURE 7–1
Hibernia Corporation Market Share, 1983–1987

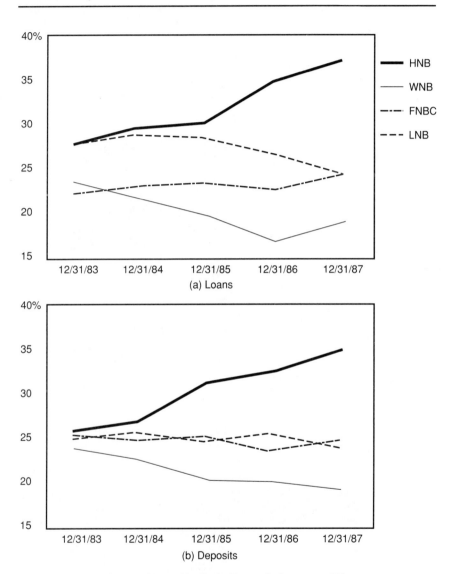

(a) Loans

(b) Deposits

New Orleans, Jefferson, Alexandria, Baton Rouge, Lafayette, and Shreveport

HNB - Hibernia National Bank; WNB - Whitney National Bank; FNBC - First National Bank of Commerce; LNB - Louisiana National Bank

FIGURE 7–2
Return on Assets, 1986

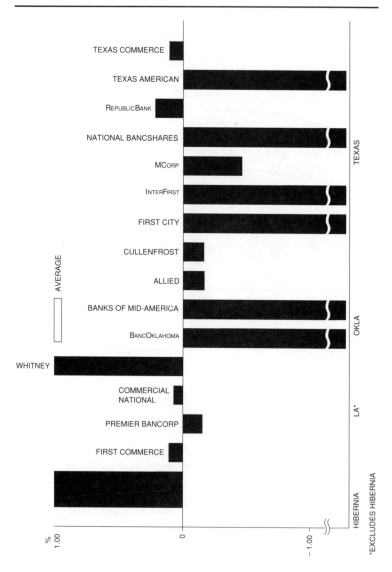

FIGURE 7–3
Return on Equity, 1986

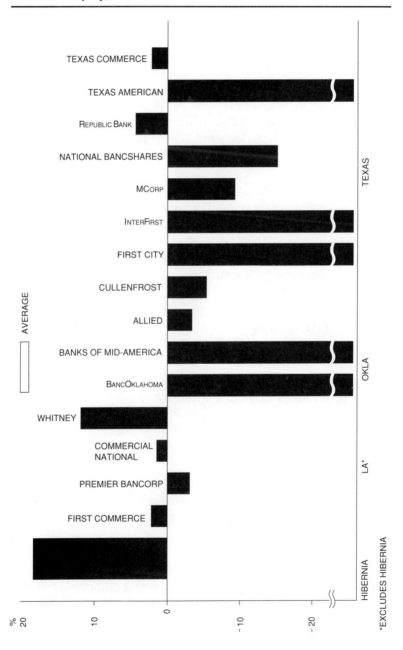

the present, Hibernia refused to be intimidated and, in fact, seized what opportunities existed. As the corporation stated in a recent annual report, "While others have made excuses, we have made strides."

THE HIBERNIA SECRET

The performance figures posted by Hibernia National Bank in recent years would be considered superb no matter in what part of the country it was located. The fact that they have been achieved in the depressed economy of Louisiana borders on the miraculous.

Of course, it wasn't a miracle that made it happen. The bank's performance has been the result of tough, aggressive, and prudent management, led by Martin C. Miler, HNB's chairman, president and chief executive officer.

Mr. Miler, now 54, came to Hibernia in 1973 from the First Union Corporation in North Carolina. When he arrived in New Orleans, he found a bank, the third largest in the state at the time, that was practically dead in the bayou. A year later the bank was making money.

"Hibernia was on its knees," Miler recalls, "and we had to introduce a whole new mentality."

He instituted a basic philosophy that has made HNB a showpiece among banking institutions:

- Enrich the stockholders.
- Focus on customer needs.
- Have superior people.

Not only was he able to make good on these objectives, they continue to govern the bank to this day.

Shareholder's Equity

Shareholders' equity totalled $287.7 million at December 31, 1987, compared to $256.2 million at December 31, 1986, and $155.3 million at December 31, 1985. The five-year compound growth rate for average shareholders' equity was 29.0 percent.

The $31.6 million increase in shareholders' equity for 1987 was due in large part to internally generated earnings.

Reported cash dividends per share represent historical amounts, adjusted for stock dividends and stock splits. Hibernia's current annual dividend rate per share is $1.04 with 1987 reported dividends per share of $1.01, equal to 41.2 percent of net income per share, compared to 39.1 percent in 1986 and 38 percent in 1985.

Shareholder's equity, as measured by book value per share, reached $15.07 at year-end 1987, compared at $13.65 and $10.99 at year-end 1986 and 1985, respectively. The market value of the company's stock remains well above book value.

Customer Needs

HNB is continually engaged in research to determine what the marketplace needs. Then, as Miler says, "we design product bases against those needs."

This was how the bank's highly successful "Tower Account" was developed and introduced in the early 1980s. This single moneymarket account has seen additional relationships "Christmas-treed" off it since then. The Tower account grew in the first quarter of 1988 by 17.6 percent over the figure from the year earlier. This product has left the competition far behind.

SUPERIOR PEOPLE

Right from the beginning of Martin Miler's tenure at Hibernia, the emphasis has been on quality performance and rewarding that performance. Miler wanted to create an environment that would attract the best people. He seems to have achieved this objective.

In this environment (Miler calls it a "meritocracy"), employees are rewarded for their performance and their contribution to the success of the bank. This statement from Hibernia's quarterly report sums up the approach rather well:

> Hibernia's people are vigorous competitors who win. At Hibernia the challenge to everyone is to achieve—to succeed while

others merely get by, to meet the highest quality standards, to reach and then expand our goals, and, most important, to provide the kind of customer focus which is essential to successful competitiveness.

Underlying Hibernia's achievements is an understanding that the keys to success are immutable. They are:

OUTSTANDING PEOPLE who have explicit destinations in their lives, who are resilient in tough times and who listen three times as much as they talk.

COMMUNICATION which allows problems to surface and makes solutions happen quickly.

GOALS which are consistently understood and executed throughout the company.

TRAINING which permits individuals to shape their own futures and enhances their performance.

OVERHEAD CONTROL to prevent dilution of their accomplishments and of our shareholders' investment.

REWARDS for high performance and for making good things happen.

A VERY LEAN HOLDING COMPANY

Hibernia is a one-bank holding company with a big difference from most bank holding companies. The holding company, Hibernia Corporation, is run by only a small staff and four senior officers.

This is because the holding company's chief executive, Martin Miler, says to have a bloated staff is a waste of money—and a potential loss of efficiency. Also, he is not an officer in the holding company's Hibernia National Bank.

MAKING STRIDES

We've seen how well Hibernia has performed and explored some of the organization's basic philosophies. Let's see how the organization, under the leadership of Martin Miler, has been able to leave the competition far behind in spite of a depressed economy.

In recent years, according to Miler, the bank's competitors "have been preoccupied with fighting fires." While they have been doing that, Hibernia has been producing because, he notes, "if you produce, you win."

In Commercial Lending. The ability to increase its loan portfolio (up to 11.7 percent in 1987) while maintaining asset quality has been a key factor in Hibernia's strength. Its rigorous process of credit approval and monitoring focuses on more than character and collateral; the bank also evaluates a borrower's business and cash flow to help assure repayment.

It would be difficult for a bank not to be involved in energy lending in Louisiana, and Hibernia certainly is into energy loans, but with a difference.

"We lend on a company's cash flow," Miler explains, "not its oil rigs and other equipment. That equipment," he adds, "is like kitchen appliances—they lose their value."

The bank does lend on proven oil and gas reserves—underscore "proven." And energy credits amount to around 8 percent of HNB's loan portfolio, which is probably the largest single concentration of loans it has.

Although Hibernia is the largest lender in Louisiana, about 40 percent of its loans are out-of-state. This process began soon after Martin Miler joined the bank.

"In 1973–1974, the bank was not in good shape," he says. "We had to broaden our loan base, and Louisiana had restrictive laws at the time." As a result, the bank looked outside the state. And over the years a network of loan production offices (LPOs) has been built.

"LPOs sometimes pick up a lot of garbage," Mr. Miler observes. However, they haven't hurt the bank "because of an efficient and persistent calling program."

The bank's handling of its loan portfolio is recognizied by many investment analysts. Recently, Keefe, Bruyette & Woods reported:

> Hibernia, with major loan segments outstanding to borrowers outside the state and in the relatively diversified New Orleans market, has fared much better than Commercial National and Premier, with more concentration in the areas of Louisiana that

are most dependent on the energy industry. The precipitous downturn of the state's economy left Hibernia's loan portfolio relatively unscathed; its ratio of nonperforming assets to total loans briefly exceeded 3 percent in 1986 and has since declined for five consecutive quarters, standing just below 2 percent at year-end (1987).

Of equal importance for Hibernia, its 125 percent reserve coverage of nonperforming loans at year-end is the highest in recent memory. This impressive record on coverage and quality of assets is due not only to its relatively favorable base within Louisiana and prudent diversifications through lending outside the state, but also to a consistently tough-minded policy on maintenance of quality.

Another factor in Hibernia's success, the Pershing Division of Donaldson, Lufkin & Jenrette notes, is that:

> Management is conservative in lending practices but aggressive in getting new business to enhance profitability. For example, the bank is currently encouraging economic development in its area to foreign firms and is keen to see increased investment in the state. It has offered to train personnel at tailor-made bases for key industries who wish to relocate. . . . In our view, Hibernia Corporation has all the essential elements in place to be a winner: it is a world class lender with a strong and growing capital base and excellent service delivery.

Because of its location, one would think that Hibernia would have plenty of Latin American loans on its books. But that is not the case; it has no lending exposure to lesser-developed countries.

When we asked Mr. Miler about LDC loans, which have hurt so many banks in recent years, and particularly in 1987 when a number of banks finally bit the bullet on their LDC exposure, he replied that early he "got scared of Latin American loans and pulled out." Smart move.

In Retail Operations. Hibernia has moved briskly ahead of its competition on the retail side, too. Perhaps the best example is its Tower account, mentioned earlier.

The Tower Service is now being used as an umbrella encompassing a broad range of financial services and benefits, including checking accounts, money market funds, telephone transfer convenience, combined statements, and lines of credit.

By expanding the concept of preferred rates, coupled with some innovative packaging of new products, Tower Service has become a valuable retail product for Hibernia. Currently, it is keeping the bank far ahead of its competitors, which find themselves continually playing catch-up.

For example, in just one year the bank has added the following products to Tower, as stated in these excerpts from material supplied by Hibernia:

Preferred-rate Credit Cards

Hibernia was first in the state to lower credit card rates when we introduced our preferred-rate cards. Tower Service customers can now apply for Hibernia Visa and MasterCard at an annual percentage rate (APR) of just 12.9%, with no card fee. Regular checking account customers who meet credit criteria can also receive cards at 15.9% APR—an attractive rate—and no card fee for the first year. Some of our competition have publicly indicated that they will not lower rates and that our strategy is one of "bait and switch." However, Hibernia's Tower Service customers have enjoyed a tradition of preferred rates; that fact is demonstrated best by the success of this product. Hibernia is serious about giving its customers the best rates possible. Our track record proves it.

Financial Freedom Account

The new income tax law phases out deductions for interest on consumer loans but still allows full deduction of home mortgage interest. Hibernia's Financial Freedom Account, another first in the state, allows customers to use that tax advantage to consolidate their borrowing needs under a revolving credit loan secured by their home equity. This service offers extremely competitive rates and the flexibility which our customers need.

Mortgage Loans

Hibernia recognized an opportunity in 1986 to offer conventional, FHA, and VA first mortgage loans for home purchases and refinancing. In addition to these traditional mortgage loans, Hibernia addressed a specialized customer need for first mortgages of $150,000 and more. Home loans at this level can be difficult to obtain from traditional mortgage lenders, but Hibernia saw the opportunity and moved into a creative new area of consumer borrowing. Two new loan production offices were opened in the New Orleans area to supplement the existing office in Baton Rouge. In addition to meeting the demand for mortgage loans, the program also allows us to sell selected loans in the open market when necessary. To strengthen ties with our valuable Tower Service customers, we offer preferred rates for both Financial Freedom Accounts and home mortgages.

THE STRATEGY PAYS OFF

As noted earlier, a number of investment analysts have recognized the solid performance being generated by HNB. But the performance is resulting in other, and rather substantial recognition. For example:

• Hibernia Corporation, with $5 billion in total assets, is the only bank holding company in Louisiana ranked A + (the highest ranking) by Standard & Poor's *Corporation Index* for long-term consistency in earnings and dividend growth.
• The growth and performance of Hibernia is evident in a ranking of banking organizations in the April 4, 1988 issue of *Business Week,* compiled by Standard & Poor's. Among the top 100 largest financial institutions listed, Hibernia was 49th in net income, 15th in ROA, 4th in ROE, 6th in net income increase, and 7th for five-year growth in earnings per share.

One element of Hibernia's success has been to follow the maxim: Operate like a business not a bank.

Obviously, the bank understands the important role played by marketing in the financial services industry. According to bank officials, Hibernia closely examines the marketplace and asks these questions:

• What do our customers want and need?

• What products and services are most attractive to them?
• Which are most profitable to us?

Where it has found areas of opportunity, the bank's literature states, "the solid strategy of the company has been to pursue our goals with the full resources necessary for success consistent with safe-and-sound banking principles."

This approach apparently is working most successfully in Louisiana for Hibernia.

PLANNING AHEAD

Planning is an increasingly important part of the managerial approach at most banks these days. But at Hibernia, planning is a way of life—even though there is no strategic planning department.

Such departments don't work, Martin Miler says, "because everyone has to be a part of the planning process." And they are at HNB. "People believe in something," he adds, "if they are part of something."

Don Beveridge described the HNB planning process in his book, *Execution is America's Might*:

> A team of key employees meets weekly to assess Hibernia's performance versus objectives. The team works as a group of navigators, checking the course and applying necessary adjustments. When corrections are called for, Hibernia can identify the situation and apply the appropriate remedy—either within a specific area or by adjusting variables of performance in other departments of the bank. Hibernia executives act as "trail bosses" of a financial wagon train pointed toward a singular destination: performance. Even as one department pauses along the way to effect repairs, the "trail bosses" maintain a steady momentum for the company as a whole.
>
> Those involved with the planning process say Hibernia creates a road map that identifies 85 percent of the terrain to be covered during the next 12 months. The remaining 15 percent requires some steering and mid-course corrections, adjustments that are applied by managers well versed in the process.

TAKING A STAND

Although this may not have much impact on its performance, it is interesting to see that Hibernia does not shy away from speaking on public issues affecting the banking industry. This is another reflection of the leadership provided by chief executive Martin Miler.

Here is an excerpt from the bank's current annual report that will give you an idea of how Hibernia gets into the middle of issues of concern to banking and the business community:

> An important issue will face Congress this spring which is critical to Hibernia and to its shareholders. The issue is whether Congress will allow banks to compete freely for financial services.
>
> A Congressional moratorium is now in effect to prevent banks from offering new services to their customers. This moratorium applies only to banks, while other financial service providers are permitted to continue their competitive advantages.
>
> This unfair and irresponsible restriction expires March 1, 1988, and we in the banking industry are working to prevent Congress from extending it. Congress should stop over-regulating our industry and modernize our banking laws.
>
> We encourage you to write to your Congressional delegation immediately, expressing support for these two important matters.
>
> • Allowing the banking moratorium to expire as scheduled March 1, 1988.
> • Passing new legislation to allow banks to regain their competitive position by offering new services such as securities, insurance, and real estate brokerage services.
>
> In the long run, these legislative changes will mean additional services for our customers and profitable business for Hibernia.
>
> Another critical issue faces not only Hibernia but the entire state of Louisiana: the urgent need for fiscal reform. We give our wholehearted support to the legislative program developed by the Louisiana Council for Fiscal Reform, which calls for:
>
> • State budget reform and fiscal responsibility, including requirements for a balanced budget.
> • Changing Louisiana tax laws to take advantage of federal income tax provisions.

- Changing tax laws to encourage creation of jobs by making Louisiana more competitive with other states.
- Increasing accountability of public spending by decreasing the size of state government and shifting new revenue sources to localities.

Louisiana's business people and its concerned citizens should rally behind these programs by asking their state legislators to adopt these fiscal reform measures . . . only by restructuring and streamlining state and local finances can Louisiana be guaranteed a much better future.

On second thought, perhaps being outspoken in the public arena has helped the bank by demonstrating to stockholders, customers, and the citizens of Louisiana that Hibernia cares.

AND MOVING AHEAD

Hibernia is not sitting still. It apparently is presently in an acquisition mode, looking at possible banking partners outside the state.

At the same time it is also looking at banks in areas within Louisiana where the bank is already located in order to increase its market share further. This seems to be a logical move since much of its growth in recent years has been to take market share away from other banks.

Hibernia is a bank guided by objectives, with the basic ones set by top management. Moreover, as Martin Miler is quick to point out, "The bank has never failed to meet its objectives."

It should also be pointed out that the objectives formulated are both practical and dynamic. After all, Mr. Miler observes, "We aren't dancing in the moonbeams."

DON'T MAKE EXCUSES

Every bank in Louisiana has had to deal with a terrible economy. One has dealt with it remarkably well.

Sure, some of the bank's success may be ascribed to luck— Why didn't other banks with demonstrably savvy management get rid of their Latin American loans a decade ago? Why didn't other banks making energy loans take a closer look at cash flows and how those loans would be paid back?

Luck, perhaps. But smart management, too.

The real key to moving forward in a depressed economy, however, is to make the most of the franchise that exists and to expand the loan or other business base.

When the overall market wasn't growing, Hibernia took market share away from the competition. This was done with good service supplied by top-notch people who were rewarded for their accomplishments, and by offering products that were based on what their customers needed.

It was done with products that also placed the bank ahead of other banks in the area.

It was done by focusing on asset quality and *not* lending when the chances of being paid back were problematical.

And it was done by formulating plans, developed by as many of the bank's staff as possible, and not engraving those plans in stone.

Hibernia also moved deliberately beyond the borders of its home state, often through the use of loan production offices in other locations. As a result, 40 percent of its lending is outside Louisiana.

Take Positive Action

The results recorded in this chapter demonstrate that it is possible to move forward even when the economy isn't. What is necessary is for a banking organization to assess the situation, coldly and factually, and then devise steps based on that assessment.

If this means fighting the competition for the available business, that is what must be done. And it can be done, with products that address the needs of customers and with emphasis placed on providing the best possible service to those customers. If your bank does not adequately service its customers, you can be sure another bank will.

It is also vitally important that a bank diversify its loan portfolio. Banks that concentrate on only one or two lending areas are asking for trouble—and often get what they ask for. It may not be easy to diversify; after all, energy lending in Louisiana was awfully good business when things were booming. Moreover, diversification does not happen overnight. Still, it is a goal that should be strived for.

The situation faced by a particular bank may call for moving beyond its basic market area to expand its business base. LPOs are certainly one way this can be accomplished. Another way may be buying service business units that deal with such products as mortgages or leases. If the business isn't where you are located, it may be necessary to reach out, if not branch out.

All of these steps are intelligent, pragmatic moves that can be taken by any bank, in any market, in any economy.

CHAPTER 8

MAXIMIZING THE MARKETING EFFORT
Glenfed Is Showing Financial Institutions, Including Commercial Banks, the Way.

Fully half of what I spend
on advertising is wasted.
Unfortunately, I don't know which half.
—*John Wanamaker*

Although news reports seem to indicate otherwise, not all thrift institutions are in trouble these days. One that is doing quite well is Glenfed, Inc., the parent company of Glendale Federal Savings and Loan Association.

There are a number of reasons for the success of this organization. Certainly a contributing factor, reflecting many of these reasons, has been creative marketing efforts that distinguish this company from the rest.

Glenfed's 1987 annual report states:

> Led by our new advertising theme emphasizing customer service and innovative products such as our 5/20 home loan, the California and Florida groups generated the highest loan volume in our history. . . . The company will build on its fiscal 1987 earnings momentum by "cross selling" multiple products to existing customers as well as attracting new customers through the quality of our service.

Norman M. Coulson, vice chairman, president, and chief executive officer, says, "We are becoming a more market-oriented company by enhancing our products, systems and procedures. And we are improving our customer service standards. We have transformed our branches into one-stop financial retail centers. Our branch people are now truly sales personnel. They aggressively market our product lines and services."

STRATEGIC RETAILING

Perhaps Glenfed's operating philosophy can be explained in the following statement:

> To our nearly 1.3 million customers, Glenfed isn't a $10 billion financial giant—but a neighborhood institution, offering checking, savings, and lending products and services—plus insurance, brokerage, and real estate-related products and services through Glenfed subsidiaries.
>
> Our operating goal: to be one of the most market-driven companies in the nation.
>
> Two notable steps toward that objective were taken in Fiscal 1987:
>
> - The development of profitable, high quality products and services—simplified and understandable to consumers—so we can build broader and deeper customer account relationships.
> - The transformation of our retail offices into one-stop financial centers, providing the services and financial products our customers want most at fair and competitive prices.
>
> Using these concepts, we build our success on "strategic retailing": We concentrate our branches in growth markets; We carefully select retail locations to avoid over branching; We focus on "core" products and services, delivered expertly by the industry's most highly motivated employees; We complement these core products with both wholesale and retail services from our subsidiaries.

WHEN YOU SAY JUMP, WE SAY, "HOW HIGH?"

Steven A. Tragash, who is executive vice president and director of marketing/corporate relations, came to Glenfed a few years ago to improve the public's conception of the organization. He first had to develop campaigns to enhance the thrift's image, showing that it was going to move with the market. Then marketing programs had to be developed.

One of the most noteworthy advertising campaigns was the "Jump" program. The theme, used as the heading for this section, proved to be extremely successful, both among customers and with Glenfed employees.

Perhaps that was the key to the effectiveness of the program—the active involvement of employees throughout the organization. Tragash explains it this way: "If we are to truly be a market driven company, our marketing efforts must go beyond our marketing staff. This program is an effort to turn each of our employees into marketers and active participants in suggesting new sales ideas. Our best resource for new and creative ideas is our employee base, and we're going to take advantage of it." He adds, "Glendale Federal is among a small group of American companies that are implementing progressive idea generation programs."

The latest campaign, going on now, builds on the "Jump" program, using former Olympic gold medalist Bob Seagren as primary spokesperson. Participants, incidentally, receive running shoes. Steve Tragash says he bought 8,000 pairs of shoes for employees (Reeboks, by the way), which must have raised some eyebrows in the accounting department when the bill first came in.

The emphasis on customer service in the advertising is tied to employee campaigns (see Figures 8–1 and 8–2). Here are some excerpts from material supplied to all employees for Glenfed's current "Jump '88—Go for Two" campaign.

> In the last fiscal year, we set out to make Glendale Federal's customer service the best that any customer could get—from any financial institution.
>
> And through our "Jump" campaign, we asked you to play a major role in the effort.
>
> You responded—with enthusiasm, hard work, and a caring attitude that has given Glendale Federal two extremely important new advantages:
>
> • A reputation for service we should all be proud of.
> • And a solid base for this year's theme: "Jump '88—Go for Two."

FIGURE 8–1

❖ GLENDALE FEDERAL

"SNEAKER"

ANNCR V/O: Glendale Federal began as a small, storefront savings and loan.

From the beginning, we...

...put our money where it belonged.

Safely in the homes and businesses of our neighbors.

In short, when customers had needs...

...we jumped to answer them.

You'll be happy to know that today, with over eighteen billion dollars in assets...

...we're still on very solid footing

TAG: We're Glendale Federal. When you say jump, we say how high?

Produced by DJMC Advertising, Inc.

FIGURE 8–2

First it was five-day approval on home loans.

Now, Glendale Federal introduces 59-minute approval* on consumer loans, up to $25,000, for just about anything else you want to buy.

And if you don't have an answer in under an hour, we'll pay the loan set-up fee.

To speed things even further, in most cases, we'll actually fund your loan within 24 hours of approval.

All in all, the fact that Glendale Federal offers guaranteed 59-minute loan approval shouldn't surprise anyone.

Because, when it comes to streamlining service, we're known for making rapid strides.

GLENDALE FEDERAL

When you say jump, we say how high?

*Loan packages submitted for approval should include a completed application and income verification. Student Loans are not included. Equal opportunity lender. © 1987 Glendale Federal Savings and Loan Association.

0 to $25,000 in 59 minutes.

Because in working as hard to build customer satisfaction as you did last year, you've made it possible for us to cross-sell our customers this year.

To say to every customer: "We want to do more for you."

By exploring all of our customers' financial needs, and meeting as many of those needs as they'll allow us, we'll be broadening our relationship with each of them.

Building a stronger relationship.

And a better future for our customers, our organization, ourselves, and our families.

Just as last year's effort to improve customer service depended on you and everybody at Glendale Federal, "Jump '88—Go for Two" also depends on you.

Because people and personal interaction are what can make cross-selling a success.

Cross-selling is a team effort—a team that extends beyond those of you working in the branches or at a DSC. It even extends beyond front-line salespeople.

The simple truth is, whether you serve customers directly, or serve the Glendale Federal people who do, how well you do your job, be it direct or support, will determine how successful we are this year.

In maintaining the high level of service that we established last year. And in expanding our relationships with our customers.

No matter if you're working in California or Florida.

In a branch, in a DSC, or a support department.

In a wholesale subsidiary or in one of our retail-oriented companies.

Service is important to every customer.

How well we work together as a team will determine how well we provide service.

And that will result in how well we do in Fiscal 1988.

TELLING EMPLOYEES ABOUT ADVERTISING

One thing that Glenfed does that few other financial institutions (or any other company, for that matter) do is to tell employees about upcoming advertising campaigns.

Here is what Glenfed told its people about its fall advertising plans:

We'll be airing two new "Jump" commercials this fall. These new commercials were created by the Advertising Department and our advertising agency, Davis, Johnson, Mogul, Colombatto, Inc. of Los Angeles, and were directed by Haskell Wexler, a noted director of commercials and cinematographer.

The first commercial will:

- Build awareness of our consumer loan products.
- Establish point of competitive difference by highlighting our quick approvals, by focusing on our 59-minute approvals of consumer loans up to $25,000 (see Figure 8–2).

The second commercial will:

- Focus on the safety and security of Glendale Federal.
- Deliver the message that Glendale Federal has become a large, successful, and secure financial institution through our dedication to customer service.
- Emphasize that Glendale Federal has safe, local investments.
- Reiterate that Glendale Federal puts money back into the community, with a high percentage of our investments in local homes and businessses.

In addition, we expect to develop additional product-related commercials with our celebrity spokesperson, Dinah Shore, later in the year.

WHO IS GLENFED?

Glenfed, Inc. is a diversified financial and real estate services corporation providing a wide range of products to consumers, businesses, and commercial customers throughout the United States.

Glendale Federal Savings and Loan Association, the principal operating subsidiary of Glenfed, Inc., is the fifth largest savings and loan in the nation, with more than $23 billion in assets and 217 branch offices in California and Florida.

Glenfed, Inc. also operates subsidiaries in 11 states engaged in commercial lending, mortgage banking, title and general insurance agency activities, discount securities brokerage, and real estate investment and development.

MAKING THE MOST OF ITS MARKET

Glenfed's two major market concentrations are in California and Florida. However, it is doing its best in all its market areas, as these statements by the organization's management make clear:

> One of the keys to that growth has been to expand prudently, but aggressively, into carefully selected marketplaces.
>
> We concentrate our branch offices in major population centers, with careful advance planning that assures a viable target market.
>
> Today, Glendale Federal and its subsidiaries do business in all 50 states. We have a physical presence or a significant customer base in 38 states. And our savings and loan network is concentrated in the two fastest-growing states in the nation—California and Florida.
>
> In California, our 107 savings and loan offices are in the 16 counties where eight out of 10 Californians live.
>
> And with the addition of the branch network of Guarantee Savings of Fresno, which Glendale Federal expects to acquire in Fiscal 1988, our California branch network will be composed of 148 offices, serving the counties in which 90 percent of Californians live.
>
> In Florida, our 66 offices serve 51 percent of the state's population, with expansion plans that will result in 74 Florida offices, serving 60 percent of the state's population.
>
> Our subsidiaries have offices in nine other states. And with the acquisition in Fiscal 1987 of the $3.1 billion residential loan servicing portfolio of Merrill Lynch Mortgage Corp. by GLEN-FED Mortgage, GLENFED'S customer base has expanded to all 50 states.
>
> The best is yet to come. Our savings and loan branches are where the future is. For by the year 2000, California and Florida will be two of the nation's three most populated states, with 48 million people.
>
> Long-range, we will focus on California and Florida. Yet we are ever aware of developing markets—in the "Sunbelt," the Northwest, and Southeast.
>
> We continue to react to changing demographics—opening new branches where prudent, and relocating offices when necessary.

A FOCUS ON PERFORMANCE

Back in the early 1980s, as deregulation came to thrift institutions, Glenfed went through a period of diversification that was less satisfactory. Now, however, it has gone back to its basics, building business around what it knows best—real estate.

The results, especially from 1984 on, have been excellent, particularly when compared to the rest of the thrift industry (see Figures 8–3 through 8–7). Of special note is Figure 8–6 which shows the scheduled items ratio, a measure used with thrifts. These items consist of loans over 60 days delinquent, loans in foreclosure, and foreclosed real estate owned; they totalled $121.9 million in 1987—0.67 percent of the Association's assets.

Donaldson, Lufkin & Jenrette Securities Corporation, in a report on Glenfed late last year, made these comments about the California based thrift institution:

An Emerging ARM Lender

An adjustable-rate-mortgage lender, in our terminology, is an institution that can originate ARMS in sufficient quantity to restructure its portfolio into a less interest-sensitive position, and then grow its portfolio through investing in ARMs. That task is

FIGURE 8–3

GLENFED, Inc. Asset Growth (in billions)

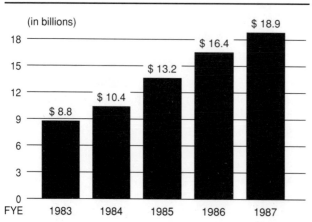

FIGURE 8–4
GLENFED, Inc. Loan Originations (in billions)

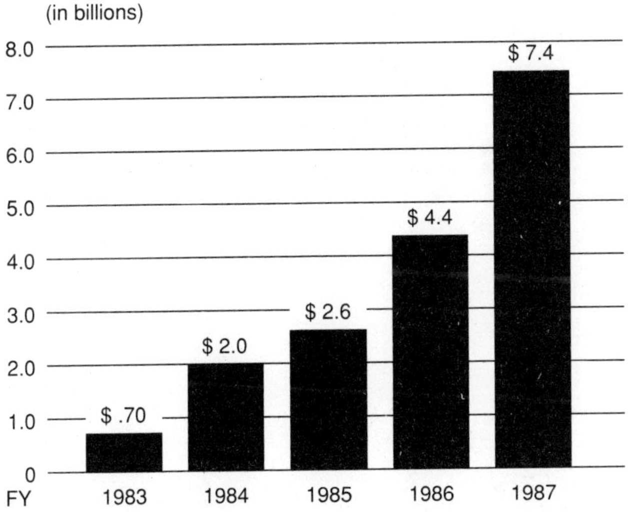

(in billions)

easier said than done. In the first half of 1986, the four largest originators of ARMs in the thrift industry created 17 percent of all ARMs written by any lender. If we add Citibank to the list, five institutions created 21 percent of all the ARMs written. Suffice it to say that originating ARMs in large quantities is not a task easily accomplished by many financial institutions.

Glenfed is now at the emerging-ARM-lender stage in its development. Its portfolio of ARMs has grown from just over $3 billion at June 1985 (or 27 percent of its interest-earning assets) to over $9 billion (or 52 percent of its interest-earning assets) at September 1987. Its one-year "GAP" ratio (a measure of interest-rate exposure, or an "unhedged" position) has narrowed from 25 percent of its assets to 8 percent of its assets over the same time. GLN [Glenfed] has just begun to enter mortgage banking by selling $400 million of ARMs in the first nine months of calendar 1987. Loan sales in 1988 are expected to be higher than sales in 1987. GLN will most likely consume some "excess" ARM production to restructure the portfolio of recently acquired Guarantee Financial, but it is likely to have excess production even after restructuring Guarantee.

FIGURE 8–5
Glendale Federal Loan Portfolio Composition

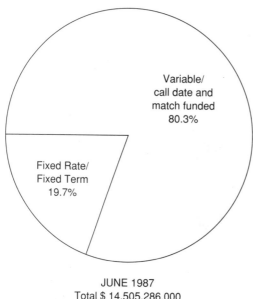

Variable/
call date and
match funded
80.3%

Fixed Rate/
Fixed Term
19.7%

JUNE 1987
Total $ 14,505,286,000

Innovation

Glenfed has been one of the more innovative lenders in attempting to turn mortgage lending into a service business, rather than into a commodity. GLN is one of several lenders to offer quick mortgage approvals by treating the mortgage as a real-estate loan rather than a personal loan. GLN calls its program its "5-20" loan approval. The company is offering five-day loan approvals, with financing to occur in 20 days from the time of application (not from the time that the information is received). The buyer must have a 20 percent down payment to qualify for the quick processing. In attempting such a quick response, GLN, we believe, is able to control its risks. GLN is able to obtain approvals quickly because it can verify the collateral (the value of the home) through use of both its own and independent appraisers. Most mortgage bankers must wait for income verification and other data (according to FHA regulations) before approval, and the process of collating the data

FIGURE 8–6
GLENFED, Inc. Scheduled Items Ratio

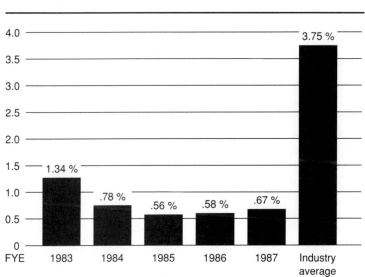

takes substantially longer than GLN's appraisal practice. GLN does not ignore the borrower's income. Income verifications are received before financing, but after the approval is given. If discrepancies arise, the loan is not financed, as we might expect.

Attention to Depositors

Glenfed's service orientation affects its philosophy toward attracting deposits as well as originating loans. Its philosophy and effort are best reflected by an advertising campaign. Normally, the measurable effect of new advertising and promotional activities is extremely difficult to observe, in our opinion. Thus, those activities are generally irrelevant to the course of a stock price. Glenfed, however, has a unique new program that deserves notice. The advertising theme is "We're Glendale Federal.

When you say "Jump" we say "How high?" Now, the slogan is cute, but what makes the program unique is that Glendale is holding "Jump" rallies for its own employees, giving out "Jump" athletic shoes (a not-so-subtle reminder) and rewarding more than one in every three employees for their performance, either in cash or in in-house recognition. The objective of the program is not only to impress its customers through advertising, but also to develop the morale and corporate culture to deliver the promised service.

Customer service does depend upon the person delivering the service as much as, if not more than, the data-processing-systems support. Motivating a clerical workforce is a difficult task because productivity is hard to measure. Tying the advertising theme with an employee-motivation program may improve the morale of employees and increase the level of service delivered by those employees. Measuring the effect of increased employee morale on earnings per share would be a quantitative chore that we do not intend to do. The effort, however, made by GLN's management to be innovative is noteworthy, whether the program succeeds in its intended goal of enhancing service or not.

Core Earnings

Core earnings have increased rapidly as GLN has improved its interest-rate spread and also has grown its portfolio of loans.

FIGURE 8–7
GLENFED, Inc. Net Earnings (in millions)

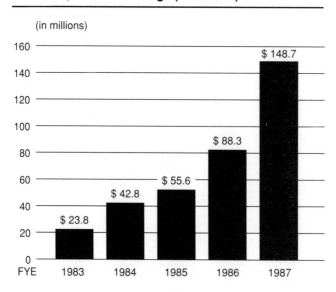

Nearly all of its earnings growth in 1986 and a large portion of its earnings growth in 1987 were attributable to the decline in interest rates, which allowed GLN to remove older low-yield loans from its books. GLN's interest-rate spread, or the difference between the rate that it receives on its loans against what it pays on its deposits, has improved from 2.15 percent at the beginning of fiscal 1986 to 2.58 percent at the beginning of fiscal 1988. Future earnings growth out of continued improvement in its spread is conceivable, but we believe that it will be difficult for GLN to improve to a level of more than 3 percent. To that degree, the most significant growth in GLN's core earnings has occurred as its portfolio has been restructured.

Asset Quality

Glenfed has been very conscientious about keeping the quality of its assets high. Glenfed's chargeoffs were .07 percent of its average assets ($.07 for every $100 lent) in 1987, up from .04 percent in 1986. Although cynics will note that chargeoffs accelerated, in relation to the high-quality regional banks, which write off .40–.60 percent, or to the high-quality thrifts, which write off .10–.15 percent, GLN's asset quality ranks among the best.

MOVING FORWARD WITH FINESSE

Glenfed has moved into the front ranks of the thrift industry in recent years; there is little likelihood that it will relinquish the position it has achieved, certainly not without making the most of its strengths.

But Glenfed's management is under no illusions that the future will be easy. Mr. Tragash, for one, looks for some fierce fighting among financial services companies over the next few years. He also observes that "what makes the difference between companies is the quality and the marketing of its services."

Obviously, Steve Tragash believes Glenfed comes out ahead on that score.

MARKETING AS A WAY OF BANKING LIFE

For the vast majority of banks, banking really is a far different business than it was, say, only twenty years ago.

Certainly, a significant part of the difference has been due to technological advances. But as much if not more is because of deregulation and the competitive factors it has unleashed, making banking a marketing-oriented industry. Unless a bank is the only game in town, or it provides a service or an expertise that sets it apart from (or above) the rest, a bank must intelligently market itself simply to keep pace with its competitors.

A true market-oriented organization has to do more than that, however. It must marshal *all* its resources in the market effort—a substantial budget, creative advertising and promotional programs, the support and participation of all levels of management, the informed involvement of customer contact personnel, and the assistance of everyone else in the company.

It is this total kind of effort that has made Glenfed such a major player among savings and loan institutions. And a number of things being done at Glenfed are activities that can be adapted and put into use by a great many financial institutions.

Keeping staff informed.   A key apsect of Glenfed's marketing is to let its employees know what is going on—with new products and services, about promotional activities and advertising campaigns.

There are several objectives for this course:

- Acquaint the staff with a bank's products and services so they can better sell them.
- Let employees know the importance management places on the marketing function.
- Develop a sense of involvement by the staff in the activities of the organization.

Some of the efforts at Glenfed concern the training of personnel in how to better sell its products and services. One of its programs, "Sales Advantage Series," provides branch office staffs with information on new products and current product promotions.

The series consists of a video tape and a manager's training guide featuring the firm's top salespeople selling the products in role-playing situations and explaining the product's benefits. In the manager's training guide, there is information about:

- The product's benefits.
- How to sell it.
- Which customers are most likely to buy it.
- What other products can be cross sold with it.
- Operational considerations in selling it.
- The firm's competitors and how their product, advertising, and marketing support compares with Glenfed.

According to officials of the thrift, before each edition of the series is prepared, they talk with Glenfed sales people to get their ideas, techniques and tips. This is done to ensure that the series is relevant to the branch sales environment and the changing training needs of its employees.

Obviously, what Glenfed does in this program demonstrates a belief on the part of the company that employees are important to the marketing effort. It also indicates a professional approach to the effort, and great attention to detail.

Cross Selling Refined.   Many financial institutions talk about cross selling, but Glenfed takes it a step or two further. In one of its brochures to employees, the institution points out that every customer is a potential new customer. Why is this so?

> Our research had indicated that our existing customers receive just 26 percent of their financial services, on average, through Glendale Federal, with an average of 1.6 accounts. And they deal with an average of 3.3 other institutions.
>
> Our goal for 1988 is to raise the average number of accounts they have with us to two—at the expense of those other institutions.
>
> How? By continuing to provide current customers with the same high level of service we established as a standard last year, while communicating to them the benefits of other Glendale Federal products and services.

Here is a program that underscores the need to cross sell

services, but backs it up with research to show how much can be accomplished.

Glenfed has mounted a marketing program that includes tasteful, interesting, and highly professional advertising (both television and print) with programs involving all the employees of the organization, and supports the marketing effort with research and well-thought-out training. This is something any financial institution can do.

CHAPTER 9

THE CREATIVE DEVELOPMENT AND MARKETING OF BANK PRODUCTS AND SERVICES
What the Signet Banking Corporation Does and How it Does It.

In business as in other
indoor sports, position
isn't everything—
but almost.
—*Richard R. Conarroe*

In 1922, shortly after the Morris Plan Bank of Richmond opened for business, the president and founder, Thomas C. Boushall, established a branch office in the Phillip Levy and Company furniture store. The idea of a branch bank office inside a retail store was too much for the other bankers in Virginia's capital city, and they complained to the state banking authorities. Within weeks the Commissioner of Banks rescinded his approval of the branch, and it was closed.

Later that same year, the bank unveiled another first, this time an effort to build deposits by selling savings stamps. The stamps were then pasted in a booklet. When the booklet was filled with stamps totalling $1.00, a savings account could be opened at the bank.

This retail-oriented approach, which also included such promotions as dropping leaflets from airplanes, was uncommon among commercial banks during the 1920s. But the approach worked and helped the bank when the country endured the hard times of the 1930s.

The pattern of innovation and customer service, in evidence from the very beginning, has been continued into present times by its successor bank, Signet Banking Corporation. The legacy of Tom Boushall lives today, carried out by its current management and staff.

WHAT'S IN A NAME

Since 1922—a relatively short period of time as banking institutions go—the bank has evolved through several name changes. From the Morris Plan Bank of Richmond, it became the Bank of Virginia, then Virginia Commonwealth Bankshares, later the Bank of Virginia Company, and, since 1986, Signet Banking Corporation.

Signet was the name chosen following the merger with Union Trust Bancorp of Maryland and planned extensions of the bank's market territory. This included the acquisition of Security National Bank of Washington, D.C. in 1987. As a result, the organization gained a presence throughout what has been dubbed the "Golden Crescent," which extends from Baltimore to Washington, south to Richmond, and east to Norfolk and Virginia Beach.

A name change has to be announced to the public, often using an advertising campaign. Signet's campaign was different, with a series of ads reaching different segments of the population that discussed the bank's purposes as well as the change in name (see Figures 9–1 and 9–2).

Obviously, calling itself the Bank of Virginia Company was no longer appropriate. Signet was selected because, among other things, it was not geographically restrictive. As was stated in the annual report for 1987, "We may have changed our name but not our commitment to providing quality service to our customers. . . ."

This commitment to quality, it is a pleasure to report, is more than a slogan at Signet.

FIGURE 9–1

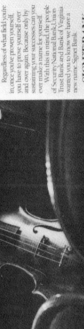

FIGURE 9–2

"After 12 years of being told hillbilly music doesn't sell, I have a hit record. And that's without compromising my style of music. Or myself."

—Dwight Yoakam, singer

It doesn't matter if you're out to become the best country singer in the world or the best bank in the region. You set a goal. Then you live by it. That's how you make a name for yourself.

With this in mind, the people of Bank of Virginia, Security National Bank and Union Trust Bank wanted you to know we have a new name. Signet Bank.

SIGNET BANK

Remember This Name, One Day We'll Be Your Bank.

Signet Bank, Virginia. Signet Bank, N.A. Signet Bank, Maryland. Member FDIC.

EMPHASIZING QUALITY

One of the keys to success in any bank's products and services is the quality of those products and services. Signet goes to great pains to ensure quality. Hardly an issue of the regular newsletters distributed to employees does not mention quality in some way or another, as this item illustrates:

> Every time a bank performs for a particular customer, the customer makes an assessment of the quality of the service received, even if unconsciously. We can think of the customer as carrying around a kind of "report card" in his or her head, which is the basis of a grading system. It is the "grades" we receive in our customers' minds that lead them to decide whether to partake of the service again or to go elsewhere.
>
> One of the obvious places to start in determining how we can earn high grades is to think about the various points of contact at which the customer passes judgement on the quality of service he or she received. The first place would be in our retail offices or branches. When customers are initially sold an account, they are sure to form first impressions about Signet. And each time they conduct business at the teller line, more impressions of our bank are formed and stored in the customer's mind.
>
> But what happens when a customer calls in with a problem or concern? This call can (and does) go to any department throughout the bank. How many opportunities are we missing to get high grades when that occurs? We've all been trained in how to handle disgruntled customers but do we really understand the importance of resolving those problems and questions? Do we even understand the importance of customers just voicing their concerns?

A QUALITY EXAMPLE

There are some similarities between Wall Street's investment banking houses and Signet Investment Banking Company: the pace is hyperactive, sometimes frantic, and everything else slows when a deal is in the works.

On Wall Street, however, top priority is assigned to closing the deal, often regardless of whether or not the client's best interests are served. Instead of endorsing this transaction-oriented philosophy geared to the quick sale for a nice profit, Signet's investment bankers concentrate on solutions to a client's goals, offering an intense objectivity rarely found in this business.

The Signet difference is paying off, says Todd Parchman, senior managing director of Signet Investment Banking Company. Since the formation of this banking subsidiary three years ago, about 45 clients in the mid-Atlantic region have taken advantage of the company's advice and expertise, resulting in over $1 million of fee income.

Parchman explains that his division complements the bank's overall corporate banking strategy. In those instances when a traditional commercial loan does not satisfy a client's complex credit needs, Signet's investment bankers can then present a menu of specialized financing options such as private replacements of equity and lower-end investment grade debt or even equity.

By capitalizing on strengths in management buyouts, acquisition-related financing, and mergers and acquisitions, this unit boasts an ever growing list of clients, ranging from a 12-store fast-food restaurant chain to a cable TV company to a manufacturer of movable office partitions. The group's biggest coup to date involves acting as agent for a Maryland developer engaged in a major acquisition—a $100 million deal.

Mr. Parchman is proud of the reputation for high caliber service that his group is establishing. "This business is quality-driven, not price-driven," he remarks, remembering a situation where both Signet and a competitor were bidding to evaluate an employee stock option plan for a large video retailer. "Although Signet's bid was more than $10,000 higher, the client selected our investment bankers to handle the valuation."

A PRODUCT AND SERVICE ORIENTATION

While Signet is often first with a new service or product, its success really depends on how it runs with the idea. A prime example of this is the credit card operation at the bank.

The bank was one of the founders of MasterCard. Being

a pioneer in this relatively new banking service has certainly helped the organization. As Robert M. Freeman, president and chief operating officer, points out, "We are the oldest bank card in existence."

He also notes that "credit cards are a valuable consumer product, but you need outstandings in order to make money." This sometimes requires a financial institution to rethink its approaches in order to build necessary outstandings or, as Mr. Freeman puts it, "rearranging the deck chairs."

Which is what Signet did.

Back in 1985 the management of the bank noticed that its solicitations for new business were slowing. This is when Signet started to work with groups, getting them to sponsor cards. Today, the bank is the second largest "affinity" bank card issuer in the country.

Working with groups, getting them to market cards to their members, was a technique just getting off the ground when the bank first got involved three years ago. Among other things, David K. Hunt, executive vice president of Consumer Financial Services, says it required the bank to move into joint venture marketing. Actually, this was a logical move necessary to the affinity card concept. After all, many groups have never used cards before so they need the kind of marketing know-how that a bank such as Signet can provide.

Also, at Signet, credit card activities are organized as a separate business. "It is important if you can isolate a product or segment it so it is possible to operate it as a going business," Mr. Hunt says. "This created responsiveness [on the part of the staff] and is a key to success."

The credit card business at Signet is a big business. The bank has more than one million cards in circulation and $1 billion outstanding.

MODERNIZING THE MORTGAGE BUSINESS

The Signet Mortgage Corporation (SMC) has entered a new phase of production that will mean a significant increase in mortgage business in the Metro-Washington area. Headquartered in Baltimore, SMC has instituted major changes that now enable the division to actively and aggressively pursue mortgage business.

"The mortgage industry is changing," says Virginia Smith, president of SMC. "What we did, what anybody did in mortgage years ago, has changed drastically. Signet needed a mortgage program that is adaptable and takes advantage of new developments in the marketplace."

A computer-based "pipeline" was designed so that SMC now has a current inventory of loans being processed. A risk management system was also designed so that the entire portfolio can be monitored on a daily basis.

Recently $25 million in existing mortgages were packaged for sale in the secondary market. This not only helped Signet reduce its provisions for loan losses, but SMC was able to retain the servicing rights on the mortgages and the resulting fee income.

SMC has also redesigned its work force to accomodate the needs of the market. Loan originators have been hired to make calls soliciting realtor and builder business.

In another move SMC has expanded its loan products to include Veterans Administration (VA), Federal Housing Administration (FHA), and Federal Housing Development Authority (FHDA) loans along with conventional loans, including Adjustable Rate Mortgages (ARMS).

The new moves have not replaced the importance of branch referrals. In fact, SMC has installed an incentive program whereby any Signet employee can earn $50 on a referral that goes to closing.

OTHER PRODUCTS AND SERVICES

An example of how Signet has been able to develop a market rapidly and effectively is its efforts in *home equity lending*.

A couple of years ago the bank decided to go all out in this quickly expanding service. According to Mr. Freeman, "We felt there was a big potential for us." This potential was helped along to a considerable degree by provisions in the Tax Reform Act of 1986.

By the end of the first year, 1986, the bank had 18,000 home equity accounts and 25,000 more at the end of 1987. Moreover, and it is a very good point, Mr. Freeman notes that "most of our accounts have been new accounts."

Equity lines of credit are sold by mail. Then the branches are given the assignment of closing the deals. Later, branch personnel try to cross sell other products. Since so many of the accounts have been new to the bank, the potential for the insititution is tremendous—and not particularly good news for the competition that finds clients leaving.

Variable Rate Mortgages.   The law was changed a few years ago allowing banks to offer mortgages where the rate of interest could change. "When the change came," Philip H. Davidson, executive vice president for planning and management information, told us, "We saw a window of opportunity and went for it."

This is another feature of Signet's mode of operation: being prepared to move into an area when the opportunity arises. It is not always easy to accomplish, much work often has to be done, and a great deal of advance planning is necessary.

Student Loans.   Many banks have been burned in lending to college students. Not Signet. "We only book those loans that are government approved," Mr. Freeman explains. "If they go bad, we get rid of them and send them to Sallie Mae" (the Student Loan Marketing Association).

There are other problems with student loans these days. For example, the government is narrowing the spread which reduces the profit margin. However, Freeman says, "If you get into the business, and you are a low-cost producer, you ought to be able to make money." This is pragmatic, hard-nosed banking. And it is working at Signet.

CHANGING PRODUCT NAMES

Signet, in all its various units, recently changed the names of many of its products. The mergers in recent years had resulted in the bank's offering similar products using different names.

The bank decided to develop standard names for these products in order to eliminate customer and staff confusion between its banking groups and, not incidentally, to better utilize advertising dollars.

For example, these names were changed:

From	To
Regular Checking	Balance Option Checking
Money Market Checking	Preferred Checking
Smart Money Market Account	Money Market Savings
Personal Credit Line	Preferred Credit Line
Equity Line	Home Equity Line
Special Edition Gold Mastercard	Gold Mastercard
Simple Interest Fixed Rate Loan	Fixed Rate Installment Loan
Simple Interest Variable Rate Loan	Variable Rate Installment Loan

Before making the changes, marketing research was conducted to determine customer sensitivity to product names. The results showed that customers think of bank products in very generic terms and really don't know and sometimes don't care what the specific service is called.

Marketing then reviewed existing product names and tried to make them descriptive, but short. The advertising campaign to announce the new names did not mention the change of name. However, the change has allowed the use of advertisements such as the one shown in Figure 9–3 for its preferred Checking Account.

By being consistent companywide with the name of its products and services, Signet has been able to reduce the cost of producing forms and sales support literature and is making staff training easier.

A SALES CULTURE

Bob Freeman tells the story of a small branch office in Maryland (formerly part of the Union Trust Bank) where sales have just taken off. It seems the branch manager, a woman who had been with the branch before it was merged into Signet, had

FIGURE 9–3

Cleverly Hidden Somewhere In This Ad Are The 8 Reasons Our Preferred Checking Account Is So Popular.

It may take you some doing, but if you study this ad long enough, you're sure to find all 8 reasons why so many people prefer our Preferred Checking Account. We don't want to give you any hints...but here comes one now. Shh.

 **(1.) Overdraft Protection**

What a sleuth. You found it—overdraft protection. This feature, along with your revolving credit account, can help to keep your balance out of the (Okay, okay, here comes a hint about how to find the next reason)..."*red*."

(2.) No Annual Fee For The First Year On a New Regular MasterCard*

So, you found the part about the free MasterCard. Okay, now it's on to reason number 3. We won't "*point it out*" for you but we'll give you "*a hand*."

 **(3.) First Order of 50 Wallet-Style Checks Is Free**

You're three for three. You're incredible.

(4.) $10 Off Your First Brokerage Trade

If you're a new brokerage customer and you'd like to call your own shots in the market, you'll like this feature. And if you'd like to get your loans at the best interest rate you can find, and then some, you just "*half*" to find reason number 5.

©1988 Signet Banking Corporation

 (5.) ½% Off On Loan Rates

That's ½% off our already competitive rates if you decide to use our convenient automatic deduction.

(6.) Free 24-Hour Banking Card

You're six for six. You must've done this before. You have, haven't you?

 (7.) Balance Build-Up Period Helps You Avoid Service Charge

When you open Signet's new Preferred Checking Account, you will have three statement cycles to increase your account balance to the point where you can avoid any regular monthly service charge.

 (8.) Balance In Your Savings Helps You Avoid Service Charge

When you keep a qualifying balance in your Signet savings account you won't be charged a regular monthly service fee on your Preferred Checking Account.

Congratulations. You have found all 8 reasons. And now that you have, you're invited to stop by any Signet Bank office, or call 800-223-4636. Certain restrictions apply. Ask for details.

SIGNET BANK

Remember this name. One day we'll be your bank.
Signet Bank/Virginia, Signet Bank/Maryland and Signet Bank N.A. Members FDIC.

developed customer service representatives, worked with tellers on customer relations and cross selling services, and generally made herself available to deal personally with customers and their problems.

The manager told headquarters officials that she saw sales as the key to recognition in the bank. It sure has got her recognized. A video has been made about the branch and how it has built business; the video is being sent around to the other branches to assist them in increasing sales.

Sales is not a four-letter word at Signet; rather, it is encouraged and built into the organization at all levels. At the same time the bank does not simply push its products. David Hunt puts it this way: "It is not our business to sell what we've got but to sell you, the customer, what you need."

USING INCENTIVES

Signet management is sold on the use of incentives to increase sales and profits and efficiency. Incentives are in place in the branches, on credit cards, in the back offices. For example, recovery people (collectors) get increments based on the amount of money collected.

The bank recently announced a special incentive program called "Budget Buster." It expands the current incentive programs, emphasizing the importance of selling to the customer. It uses a combination of cash awards and prizes.

However, the use of incentives, Mr. Freeman told us, shifts the emphasis from motivation to control. "Our systems are monitored," he said, "to make sure that everything is operating satisfactorily." He is particularly concerned about incentives to loan officers. Without adequate controls, he cautioned, incentives in this area can cause trouble.

A MATTER OF PRICING

In recent years, the bank has moved aggressively to counter the competition by introducing a tiered pricing structure, with account balances determining the rates.

The financial impact of this change in 1986 was negligible. In 1987, however, a decrease in interest income of approximately $11.7 million, with additional fees of approximately $5.4 million, offset a portion of this negative impact. With volume improvement and the repricing of large blocks of long-term consumer certificates of deposit used to fund the portfolio, interest expense was reduced by about $9.0 million. This more than offset the remaining negative impact of reduced interest income.

At present the bank has consistent pricing of products throughout the system. However, because Signet operates in different markets, a closer look at this aspect of the business is being made.

"We are in many markets," David Hunt notes. "We must have the flexibility to have discrete marketing in the various segments. It is legitimate to have different strategies in different markets. It is important to look at the individual market."

This is a current priority at Signet. It is very possible that different prices may be set for, say, a certified check in different locations, such as the District of Columbia and Wytheville in southwestern Virginia.

MANAGING THE MARKETS

With the completion of its initial "Golden Crescent" strategy resulting from the acquisition of Security National, management decided Signet should be reorganized to take advantage of the opportunities that the markets afforded it. It was felt the Corporation needed to be organized along market lines rather than as individual banks.

The realigned management mirrors three principal markets by forming a Virginia Group, a Maryland Group, and a Metro-Washington Group. In addition, a Capital Markets Group was formed and is comprised of the Corporation's treasury function, investment portfolio management, investment banking, and securities dealing activities.

This strategic move has helped Signet to maximize its market penetration within the "Golden Crescent."

Development of the three markets is expected to provide Signet with opportunities for continued growth, greater productivity, and increased profitability—and at the same time offer customers more convenience and quality banking services.

Signet in 1988 has traveled a long way from the Morris Plan Bank of Richmond. Yet the bank continues along the same route it took right from the beginning in 1922—a route leading to the development and marketing of products and services its customers want and need.

MAKING THE RIGHT MOVES

Creativity in the development and marketing of a bank's products and services is an almost essential ingredient for a bank's success these days.

Product development was once the sole province of manufacturing companies; banks did not have to be concerned about such mundane matters. As most banks are well aware, those days are long past.

Competitive pressures are not only causing banks to come up with new products and services, they are requiring banks that wish to move ahead of the pack to examine, redefine, and even revise existing products and services to better satisfy the needs of the marketplace.

Look at what Signet has done with its credit card business. A major player in this nontraditional banking service early on, the banking company continues to explore new ways to make the business productive. The affinity card has provided a great boost and has breathed new life into the business for Signet as it makes the most of this fresh credit card concept.

Who knows what the next development or advance in the credit card area will be? However, you can be sure that Signet will be in the forefront when that development comes along. The reason: People at the bank continue to be alert to the market changes and trends, and are ready to explore new directions.

Any bank should look at any and all of its products and services periodically to determine if improvements can be made in their design. And while doing this, a bank should examine the marketing and delivery of those products as well.

Because of the advances in technology, this latter aspect— delivery—probably offers some of the best opportunities for improvements. If changes can be effected in how a service is delivered to a customer, or in the way it is processed, the usefulness to customers may be enhanced and the costs to the bank (as well as to the customer) may be lowered.

A bank that can accomplish such things is far better prepared to stay a step or two ahead of its competition than one that doesn't even try.

Consider the case of the automated teller machine (ATM). What a terrific idea, the epitome of what technology can do for customers. It provides an opportunity to enhance dramatically the distribution of banking services by satisfying customer desire to have those services more conveniently and with little delay.

Unfortunately, the public did not see things that way. They did not flock to those first ATMs. In fact, it was a common sight a few years ago to see lines of customers waiting for tellers while an ATM near the entrance to the bank stood idle. Many people were not comfortable with the new technology and so they simply ignored it. Meanwhile, banks saw their rather considerable investment in equipment lose money.

Inducements were offered to entice customers to the machines—awards for first use, fees for using live tellers. Some of these things helped, though often just marginally. The real advance in their usage came, however, when banks began to place ATMs on or near college campuses. Young adults were at home with high-tech; they found the machines convenient and easy to use. And they paved the way for ATM acceptance by their parents.

Clearly, those early marketing efforts for ATM usage were not directed to the right target.

A different case involves home banking. Here was another advance that customers would love. However, many of the programs that were instituted a few years ago never got off the ground. The concept was creative enough, but it overlooked one criterion for a successful service—it must satisfy a need or, failing that, create one.

Up to the present time, home banking apparently has done neither. In all fairness, it is possible that the marketing efforts employed were improperly directed. In any case, home banking remains a product in search of a market.

This is an exciting time for the banking industry. It is also probably more challenging than ever before. New and/or better products and services are most important as banks try to meet the challenges they face. Successful banks will need to use all their creative resources to provide the kinds of products and services a sophisticated and expanding marketplace will accept.

PART 4

BANK SPECIALIZATION

The banking business used to be so simple, so uncomplicated. A bank would take in deposits, loan out money, and, if it figured its margins right, it made money.

Today, for most banks, it's a different ballgame—pardon us—a different banking game. Full service banks are, in fact, full of services, with new ones seemingly being added almost daily. But the very completeness of many of these financial organizations has opened the door to specialization.

There always have been specialized banks, of course. But now there are often unique features or aspects of some of the specializations. Not only that, some of the specialized banks stand out, not only for what they do, but for how they do it.

This certainly is the case with Republic New York Corp., which is rather like an old-world private bank, flowering in the midst of a high-tech financial marketplace. But more than that, the thrust of its growth—and the reason for much of its profitability—is deposits. It is an approach that governs the bank's activities, including its balance sheet management.

This is also true of Northern Trust Company in Chicago. Here is a bank that offers full commerical bank services, but much of its drive—and a good deal of its profits—comes from its trust operations. And, as you will see, the bank concentrates only on certain trust businesses, not all. This is a bank that knows where its trust expertise is, and where it is not.

A somewhat different kind of specialization is explored in niche banking, a segmentized market approach, used in general, by small banks, that has proven highly successful in this day of the mega-bank. The two banking companies profiled are growing and doing well, so well that they are already prime candidates for acquisition. Probably by megabanks.

CHAPTER 10

FINDING A NICHE— AND MAKING THE MOST OF IT
Lincoln Bancorp and Point West Bancorp Have Found Their Own (Profitable) Banking Worlds.

Don't find fault.
Find a remedy.
—*Henry Ford*

Banking companies that aim at a certain segment of the financial market, or perhaps a segment in a special location, are sometimes called "boutique" banks. They are specialty shops, usually catering to a limited clientele.

While that term is, in many ways, quite appropriate, it can also be a turn-off. "Boutique" can denote aloofness, a feeling of superiority . . . or inferiority.

Many bankers who head up such focused financial firms hate the term boutique. Rather, they would describe their banks as operating within a specific niche. This, too, is an accurate description and without the negative connotations.

Regardless of what they are called, these banks are generally small to medium in size, many are relatively new on the scene, a surprising number are making money and they can be found in just about every section of the country. Also, and not always incidentally, they are often desirable takeover prospects.

There have always been specialty banks, of course. Some of them have grown and prospered, broadening their customer bases to become large, full-service financial institutions.

In recent years, however, there has been a great increase in the number of banks geared to servicing a particular market niche. One reason, and perhaps the main reason, for this has been the trend toward consolidation and larger banking entities. It has been perceived—and often proven—that certain customer segments are not adequately served by such institutions. As a consequence, new banks have been found to do precisely that.

Specialty banks can focus their resources on the needs of their particular customers. Because they limit the range of services, they often need fewer employees and only one or two offices. Therefore, overhead is reduced. Many can reach profitability more quickly than bigger banks. And, with the use of correspondents and/or packaged programs, they can expand services in some instances without adding appreciably to their costs.

In this chapter we will focus on two niche banks that happen to be located in different parts of California. It would have been just as easy to select a bank in Pennsylvania or Illinois or Missouri. But California is a state where niche banking has become almost an art form; so California, here we come.

POINT WEST BANCORP

Thayer T. Prentice, transplanted from Bradford, Pennsylvania, was an officer with the Bank of California when he decided the time was ripe to start his own bank in 1979. A lot of California banks were centralizing operations and moving further away from their customers; the further away they got from the customers, the lower the level of service. The big banks were opening doors for local banks who could offer both good service and specialized services.

Five of his clients were interested in the possibility of chartering an independent banking company. After five more investors were found, Prentice and his associates opened the Point West Bank, located on the outskirts of Sacramento, in 1980.

The game plan was to focus on business firms with sales in the $1 million to $20 million range. Eight years later that game plan is still being followed, with most of the bank's 1,200 commercial customers in the $2–$10 million range.

The market was selected because the organizers are all from the Sacramento area. But is was particularly appropriate, Mr. Prentice says, because Sacramento happens to be "the fastest growing area in the United States." He also notes that "the quality of life is good here."

Today Point West serves its business customers through approximately 2,000 accounts. Individual checking accounts are offered, but only to principals of businesses that deal with the bank. The bank currently has some 2,800 checking accounts, 1,000 of them for individuals. All of the customers are in the Sacramento area, with 97 percent of them within a 10-mile radius of the bank's headquarters office and a single satellite branch. These customers are served by 110 full-time employees; 20 percent of that total are officers.

The bank turned the profit corner in 1984 and has been moving up ever since. As Table 10–1 shows, the bank is doing rather well, although its goals are not always met. One figure not shown on the chart is its capital, which has doubled since 1980 from $5.5 million to nearly $11 million. In addition, the bank is in the top 50 percent of California banks in yield as

TABLE 10–1
Point West Bank Key Ratios and Balances, 1987

	Budgeted December 31	Actual December 31
(1) Earnings Per Share	$2.31	$2.47
(2) Return on Beginning Equity	13.83%	14.79%
(3) Return on Average Assets	0.80%	0.86%
(4) Capital Ratio	6.62%	7.13%
(5) Loan to Deposit	82.35%	75.88%
(6) Secondary Reserve	17.00%	22.89%
(7) Asset Growth	21.11%	13.97%
(8) Loan Growth	22.02%	5.35%
(9) Deposit Growth	21.70%	14.05%
(10) Total Assets	$175,000,000	$164,681,078
(11) Net Income	$ 1,270,000	$ 1,358,442
(12) Loan Loss Reserve	0.85%	1.05%

assets. Its cost of funds is low, and its net interest margin is high.

The headquarters office, Mr. Prentice feels, symbolizes his bank as an innovator. Designed by local architects and built by a local construction firm (both customers of the bank), the building is modern yet utilitarian.

Now about five years old, the building is indicative of "a new style of financial service that must emerge from a deregulated banking environment. Today a bank must combine its traditions and strengths with responsiveness and flexibility."

Point West is geared to serving customers within the framework of its state charter. Mr. Prentice points out that, in California, state-chartered banks can offer some nontraditional services such as real estate investment consulting.

The bank tailored a money market account exclusively for its business customers. This has attracted more deposits from current customers and brought in a number of new customers. Not so incidentally, the Point West president adds, the account "has proven to be very profitable."

Most of what the bank offers are traditional commercial services, "but better." Since it does little advertising in the media (except occasionally in local trade journals), it does not have this expense to contend with. As a result, Mr. Prentice says, the bank pays a premium on business accounts.

One service it does not offer, which might seem a natural for a bank serving business customers with above average resources, is a trust department. "We actually looked at the possibility of opening a trust unit but decided not do it," Mr. Prentice observes. "The break-even point in the trust business is too high."

Important Differences

Two years ago the bank converted its data processing operation to a fully automated in-house system. This system allows management to pull information together so it can look at a customer's entire business relationship with the bank.

Thayer Prentice's office is a glassed-in area right off the main banking floor. When we walked into the office earlier this year, we noticed that there was no monitor in the room—a feature on most of the desks in the rest of the bank and in the offices of most bank executives these days.

"I don't believe the president of the bank should have a terminal," he explained. "My time is better spent having direct contact with people—both staff and clients."

While the emphasis at Point West is on service and good customers relations, the profit picture is by no means overlooked. "We review accounts at least annually," Prentice told us. "If a customer is unprofitable, we tell him we'll have to raise our prices to him." In most, but not all, instances the customer increases his business with the bank.

Also, as good as they are, the services are not always free. For example, the bank was the first in its area to charge a fee for granting a commercial loan.

Interestingly, assets are still funded with core deposits (deposits other than jumbo certificates of deposit). This is contrary to current trends, but it allows the bank to maintain a healthy net interest margin.

Where will Point West go from here? It already is an attractive takeover prospect. And it may be more attractive in the future. Probably within the next year or so, the bank will issue stock and offer it to the public. In fact, it already has engaged a major securities firm to explore this possibility.

In the meantime, the bank continues to move forward, meeting its objectives. Perhaps this can be summed up best by Thayer Prentice's statement which appeared in the bank's annual report:

> Point West Bank continued to focus on meeting the financial and management services needs of Sacramento's businesses. We owe our success to the support of our shareholders, Board of Directors, and the Sacramento business community. And, we believe there is a tremendous opportunity for Point West Bank's continued growth in the Sacramento marketplace. We are well capitalized, well organized, and well staffed. We understand the needs of the business market and have the flexibility to respond to those needs in a timely and unique manner.

LINCOLN BANCORP

About 400 miles south of Sacramento on busy Ventura Boulevard in the Los Angeles suburb of Encino is Lincoln Bancorp. Lincoln was incorporated in California on September 3, 1981, and operates as a bank holding company. Its sole subsidiary, Lincoln National Bank, opened for business on April 14, 1982.

With a regional office in Beverly Hills, California, Lincoln National provides wholesale commercial banking to small- and medium-sized business, business entrepreneurs, professionals, and other high-net-worth individuals. Lincoln National's market area consists of greater metropolitan Los Angeles as well as the Orange County metropolitan area of southern California, with its primary focus being the affluent business and residential areas of Beverly Hills and the San Fernando Valley.

Lincoln National's marketing philosophy is to provide high-quality, customized banking services to its target clientele. This high-quality, personalized approach has allowed the Bank to attract customers from a wide variety of manufacturing, wholesaling, and service businesses, as is reflected in the increase in its asset base from $43 million at December 31, 1982, to over $301 million at December 31, 1987.

As can be seen from Tables 10–2 and 10–3, this six-year-old bank is doing rather well in one of the most competitive banking markets in the country. Incidentally, the bank posted its first profits just five months after it started, in September 1982; and it has shown a profit every month since then.

TABLE 10–2
Lincoln Bancorp Financial Ratios

	1987	1988
ROA	0.91%	0.88%
ROE	13.74%	14.74%
Net Interest Margin*	6.50%	6.67%
Net Loan Losses to Avg Loans	0.51%	0.41%
Allowance to Gross Loans	1.54%	1.52%
Equity to Assets	6.73%	4.24%

*Before loan loss provision.

TABLE 10–3
Lincoln Bancorp Selected Balance Sheet Data

	1987	*1988*
Total Assets	$ 300,959,336	$ 241,952,517
Interest-earning assets	237,254,508	168,201,432
Interest-bearing liabilities	(127,257,027)	(90,976,039)
Loans, Net	145,544,148	107,583,603
Allowance for loan losses	2,274,537	1,664,327
Deposits	279,653,814	229,645,007
Shareholders' equity	20,249,507	10,263,214
Net Income	2,116,360	1,401,382
Book value per share	$7.88	$6.87

The bank's solid performance record has been recognized by the prestigious *Findley Reports*. This publisher of detailed analyses of banking operations has awarded Lincoln National Bank a "Q Quality Rating" and recognized the bank as a "Premier Performing Bank" every full year of its operation.

Why has Lincoln been so successful? We asked president and chief executive officer, John J. Keating, this question. "Big banks have a lot of turnover," he pointed out. "Loan officers are always changing jobs, moving to new offices. This is not the case at smaller, independent banks. Customers have direct access to decision makers."

There are plenty of other reasons, of course. For one thing, the bank's overhead is low (the headquarters office is on one floor of a nondescript office building on Ventura Boulevard), without layers of unproductive management. The bank does no advertising; customers are brought in through referrals and recommendations from CPAs. In addition, the bank tries to keep itself as lean and as flexible as possible. For example, it uses a service bureau to supply necessary automation.

But the main reason for its success, according to Keating, is that "we are doing as well as we have been because the big banks aren't doing their job. We have good people, but it's more a function of the incompetency of the larger banks" with which Lincoln competes. "They're doing such a miserable job of servicing that segment of the market."

One investment firm, Securities Investor Protection Corporation, credits much of Lincoln's success to its interest rate sensitivity:

> Lincoln National's loan portfolio is almost entirely made up of commercial and industrial loans which are fully floating with the prime rate. Nonetheless, the Investment Committee continuously monitors the bank's sensitivity to changes in interest rates and attempts to insulate the bank from excessive interest rate risk. An analysis of Lincoln National's interest rate exposure provides a very good indication of its asset/liability posture. At September 30, 1987, the Bank's one-year cumulative interest rate sensitivity gap—the difference between interest rate sensitive assets and interest rate sensitive liabilities that reprice or mature within one year—was a positive $155.5 million or 55 percent of total assets. A positive gap position is deemed favorable in a period of rising interest rates. Because of this positive interest rate gap, a ½ point increase in the prime rate will currently add anywhere from $30,000 to $50,000 per month to Lincoln's earnings.
>
> Obviously, a falling interest rate environment would not necessarily be a favorable development for a financial institution with a large positive gap position and immediately adjustable interest rates. However, Lincoln National has mitigated this problem by funding its growth primarily through interest-free demand deposits rather than fixed rate CDs. As of September 30, 1987, demand deposits accounted for 51 percent of total deposits and were comprised primarily of compensating balances from businesses and deposits from title and escrow companies. Because of the way Lincoln National positions itself from an asset/liability standpoint, it is our belief that modest swings in interest rates, either up or down, will have a negligible effect on Lincoln's net income.

A Cue From The Board

When the bank was founded, the board of directors consisted of 14 members; today there are seven. One of the founders, holding company chairman Steven C. Good, a partner in a California accounting firm, had strong business development goals.

John Keating, who is also chairman of the bank, was hired away from Union Bank, then owned by a British bank. Keating points out that he was not the board's first choice. However, he has proven to have been a good choice since he also has strong business development skills. He also brought with him several other Union executives as well as clients.

The active involvement of the board has continued. In the bank's annual report it is noted that the board has generated positive, tangible results. "In addition to their daily business activities," the report states, "they have devoted numerous hours on various committees. Equally important, they continue to be responsible for referral of new business to the bank, representing almost 15 percent of the bank's total deposits."

Keating expressed concern about the status of bank directors. He noted that directors' insurance that is currently available is "not satisfactory," explaining that directors are liable for federal suits. As a result, he said, bank directors must rely too heavily on the "integrity of the bankers who are running the bank."

Emphasis on Lending and Service

John Keating described his bank as "deposit-driven. Our basic premise is still to bring in those demand deposits and everything else will take care of itself, especially those earning figures," he noted. However, the bank also excels in both customer service and in the lending area.

The 44-year-old CEO observed that most small banks that get into trouble do so because of their loans. At Lincoln, great efforts are taken to stay out of trouble. "We turn down five or more loans for every one made," Keating said.

The bank has gotten into the mortgage lending business in order to generate fees. All mortgages put on the books have adjustable rates (ARMS). Moreover, the mortgage portfolio is fully hedged.

In common with Point West Bancorp in Sacramento, Lincoln does not compete on price but on service. For example, customer deposits are often picked up by the bank's courier.

There are currently about 3,000 accounts, mostly business, but some from individuals. These accounts are monitored for profitability. However, Keating said, "We try to do our homework so that they don't become unprofitable."

He observed that there is plenty of business in the bank's market area. "Most prospective customers," he said, "are unhappy with their present banking relationships."

When it was pointed out that there also is plenty of competition in the area, he seemed unconcerned. "Sure, but I do a better job."

Is There a Future for Lincoln?

There certainly seems to be, although it may not be as an independent bank. John Keating wants to build the assets of his bank to close to $1 billion by 1991, the year when New York banks will be able to establish branches in California. With assets now around $300 million, that's a rather tall order.

One way to accomplish this, of course, is to buy one or more banks, something that Keating is looking into. He would like to acquire banks in Los Angeles County with between $100 million and $200 million in assets although there are no specific targets. At this point in time, he says, "Greed hasn't overcome ego."

Another reason Keating wants to increase Lincoln's asset base, of course, is that the bank will be more attractive to a bank outside the state. But that's three years away.

OTHER AREAS, OTHER NICHES

Success stories similar to Point West and Lincoln Bancorp are being duplicated in many other parts of the country—and with seemingly greater frequency.

Powder Mill Bank

New banks in New Jersey are opening at a faster pace than ever before. In 1987, for example, filings for 21 new banks were accepted by the state's Department of Banking; 15 charters were approved, and 8 banks opened for business. Most of those banks could be classified as niche banks.

While perhaps not strictly a niche bank, Powder Mill Bank, located in Parsippany, in the northern part of the state about

25 miles from New York City, was established to serve the local area, both business firms and individuals. However, it is an example of how a bank, focusing on a particular market, can succeed in a highly competitive area.

Powder Mill Bank (a mill that supplied gunpowder during the Revolutionary War once stood on the site) opened its doors June 29, 1987. Currently it has over $30 million in assets and about 1,700 checking and savings accounts. Sixty percent of its 400 or so Powder Mill shareholders use the bank's services. Its initial stock offering, $4.75 million, was oversubscribed. The stock, originally $5 per share, was selling at $7.50 per share a year later.

According to President and CEO Charles J. Stancil, a banker with 20 years of experience, the bank will be profitable next year.

The incorporators (which include a congressman and a local automobile dealer) felt that the area needed its own bank. They seem to have been right. Stancil says people are getting sick of the bigness of banks, sick of red tape. In fact, he does not believe the big banks in the area really give his bank any real competition.

He attributes the success of his bank to the personalized service provided to customers, pointing out that "none are too small or too big" for Powder Mill Bank. To provide better service, undoubtedly, three branches, all within 10 miles of the main office, are expected to open shortly.

Will the bank be a candidate for a merger? Who knows, but the charter forbids one for five years.

MAKING THE MOST OF A SPECIALTY

As the examples of niche banking profiled in this chapter clearly demonstrate, there is a place for specialty-focused, limited service banks in today's financial environment.

This has always been the case for some in other kinds of merchandising. There are specialty furniture stores (bedding, children's furniture), food shops (stores for cheese, ice cream), computer stores (there is one in New York which sells only laptop computers). So the fact that this is the situation in banking should not be so surprising.

The phenomenon is caused, of course, because of the trend toward consolidation in banking with ever bigger and bigger banks. The fact that bigger is not always better has opened the door for niche banks.

Not every bank that has opened to serve a particular market segment has succeeded. In fact, all too many are being closed by the FDIC these days because of financial difficulties.

There are several things that can be done before a bank is chartered to improve its chances of success.

Obviously, the bank should be adequately capitalized. Since this is a function of the chartering process, it probably can be assumed that the regulatory authorities, either at the state or the federal level, are convinced that the capital is sufficient.

The regulators, of course, look at a variety of other factors—the people incorporating the bank, the proposed board, the senior management, the market, the competition. But still some banks fail.

Based on the niche banks that are prospering, however, there seem to be several items that should be addressed *before* a bank is organized and a charter is sought:

Market Segment

There have to be potential customers in the quantity and quality necessary for the bank to grow. If a bank is going to go after the small business market, are the number of firms in the area enough to keep the bank afloat? Are there indications that existing financial institutions are not or cannot properly serve these customers?

Studies should be done to determine the marketability and to evaluate the competition the new bank will face. If the organizers can assure that when the bank opens it will have a number of solid customers, so much the better.

Experienced Management

It's one thing to say "Let's start a bank." It's another thing to manage a bank. Any bank, and certainly one that will address a specific segment of the market, must have experienced, able bankers who know how to run a bank and how to deal with the kinds of problems with which all new banking firms must deal. You will notice that in every case mentioned in this chapter, the chief executive (and many of the chief subordinates) are all highly qualified bankers.

Business Development Skills

Also important is the marketing expertise of people within the bank and on the board. If there are no people with marketing ability involved in the new bank, it won't be able to get very far.

A Commitment to the Bank

Not every new bank can hope to turn a profit within the space of a few months as Lincoln Bank did. It may take two or more years. Those involved with the bank must be prepared to stick with it for a significant period of time. Without such commitment, the bank has little chance of survival.

GROWTH MANAGEMENT

The banks profiled have grown, not explosively, but at a measured pace. Growing too fast can cause problems, leading to underwriting difficulties, and eventually to losses.

That seems to be what happened at the National Enterprise bank in Washington D.C. (which has now affiliated with the First Interstate System). Organized by former Federal Reserve Governor (and former banker) Jeffrey Bucher in 1982, the bank was established to serve the financial needs of business and service professionals in the District of Columbia—lawyers, accountants, consultants, and others.

National Enterprise showed a profit in 1985. In fact, even after difficulties selling its initial stock offering, which delayed the bank's opening until August 1983, the assets of the bank grew to more than $50 million in just over two years.

But then troubles began to surface. A loss was posted in 1986, and the bank's first president and chief executive officer resigned. Assets fell to $42 million and an $8 million loss was reported for 1987.

Bank officials say that the cause of the bank's problems was poor underwriting standards. However, they say these standards have been shored up and the turnaround process is nearly complete. Although a new chief executive has been in place for over a year, the bank still reported a loss in the first quarter of 1988.

This story shows that without careful planning, and even more stringent controls, a bank focusing on a specific market can get into deep trouble—and in a rather short period of time.

Prospects for niche banks are bright indeed. But the risks exist, as they do throughout the banking industry. Fortunately, steps can be taken to guard against those risks.

By carefully addressing these items, and following through on them, a niche bank has a good chance of making it. When you consider the potential to the organizers, the investor, and the management, a new niche operation can be most profitable. And, if the bank is successful, it may also become a takeover candidate—which also can be a profitable proposition.

CHAPTER 11

BUILDING TRUST
Chicago's Northern Trust Corporation May Be Waiting for Its Rewards; It Has Always Known What to Do with Its Trust Department.

Today, bank failures only
mean that, like the railroads,
some bankers are just waiting
around for their virtue to be
rewarded.
—John Naisbitt, Megatrends

Because of the self-imposed hit it took with its Latin loans, Northern Trust Corporation in Chicago lost money last year.

But not the trust unit. Trust fees were up substantially, with trust fee income increasing a solid 21 percent over 1986 to a record $180.3 million (see Figure 11–1).

This kind of performance has been going on for a number of years. It has been the core business of Northern Trust and it has nurtured an ethical culture throughout the ranks of the organization. The trust business and that culture combined to help see the bank through some difficult days in the early 1980s when it found itself saddled with more Penn Square participations than it wanted—or needed.

The trust business is also instrumental these days in spreading the good word about Northern Trust around the country, particularly in ventures in Arizona, Florida, California, and most recently, in Texas.

The bank's three major trust areas are master trust, personal trust, and correspondent trust services. Ann Byrne, a senior vice president and chief financial and administrative officer of the Trust and Financial Services Group, points out

FIGURE 11–1
Trust Fee Growth (in millions)

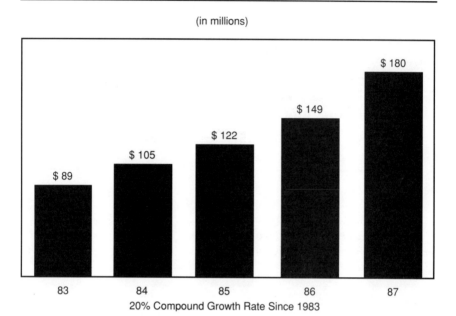

(in millions)

$ 89 — 83
$ 105 — 84
$ 122 — 85
$ 149 — 86
$ 180 — 87

20% Compound Growth Rate Since 1983

that Northern Trust once had a corporate trust services department, but got out of that business "because it was not a business
we knew that much about."

Today, according to Ms. Byrne, Northern Trust is the sev-
enth largest bank in the country in terms of trust assets, third
in personal trust (an area many large banks ignore), and either
second or third in master trust, depending on which measurement is used.

Van R. Gathany, executive vice president and deputy head
of the Trust and Financial Services Group, observes that trust
work has been important to the bank since it was established in
1889. "It has always had the resources and it has always hired
good people."

This emphasis on people is echoed by other senior trust
officers. "The successful company," says James J. Mitchell, executive vice president responsible for the Trust and Financial Services Operations and Systems Group, "is the one that can get
the right people into the jobs . . . this company is organized about

people." He also notes that the bank works at this by doing unique things to attract new people, such as "adopting" a high school and helping to solve problems at universities in the area.

Jeffrey Wessel, an executive vice president who heads the Corporate Financial Services Group, notes that Northern Trust has a higher percentage of college graduates in the back office areas of its trust operations than do other banks. Among other things, he says, this allows the bank to "respond to more opportunities."

PERSONAL TRUST

The foundation of Northern Trust's trust business is Personal Trust Services, although this is no longer the largest portion of its business.

Today, the bank administers more than $18 billion in personal trust assets, ranking in the top five bank managers of personal trust assets nationwide (see Figure 11–2). A few years

FIGURE 11–2
Personal Trust Asset Growth (in billions)

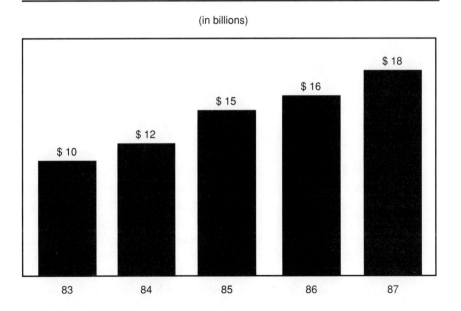

(in billions)

| 83 | 84 | 85 | 86 | 87 |
| $ 10 | $ 12 | $ 15 | $ 16 | $ 18 |

ago, President David Fox points out, "We merged our personal banking and discount brokerage areas into the trust side of the business to bring together all marketing and service delivery to individuals."

One of the few banks in the country to take this approach, it underscores, Fox adds, "our objective of capturing business at all stages of a client's life cycle, from the wealth accumulation stage to estate planning needs."

Commenting on the bank's moves beyond Illinois, Mr. Fox says that "Early this year we established a trust company in California, with offices in Santa Barbara and Los Angeles, with plans to add a third office in San Francisco. California is a key high growth market for wealthy individuals as well as for master trust services."

CORRESPONDENT TRUST

The second line of trust services provided by Northern Trust is the trust fee work it does for correspondent bank trust departments, which includes investment advisory and back office functions such as custodial and accounting services. What the bank is doing is wholesaling its skills in this area and leveraging off economies of scale.

"This is a relatively new dimension for us," David Fox states. "But the results have been dramatic as our assets under custody have grown to $12 billion within the last three years." (See Figure 11–3.)

A MASTER OF MASTER TRUST

The third and largest segment of Northern Trust's trust business is master trust. A master trust is an arrangement whereby the bank acts as trustee, cash manager, and securities custodian for large pools of assets with multiple investment managers.

The growth in these assets has been substantial. At the end of 1987 Northern Trust had $106 billion of assets under administration for its 231 master trust clients (see Figure 11–4). There was an impressive 19 percent growth from new business

FIGURE 11–3
Depository Custody Services Asset Growth (in billions)

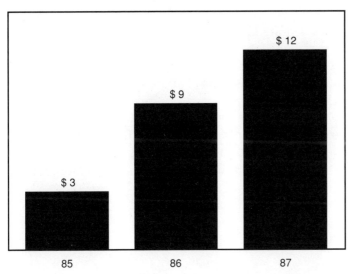

(in billions)

$ 12

$ 9

$ 3

85   86   87

FIGURE 11–4
Master Trust Asset Growth (in billions)

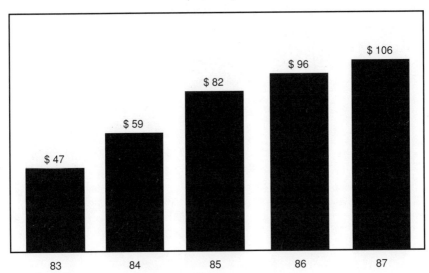

(in billions)

$ 106

$ 96

$ 82

$ 59

$ 47

83   84   85   86   87

in the first quarter of 1988, increasing the client base to 245 and adding $20 billion in assets.

Northern is the market leader in terms of number of clients, with a market share of 15 percent, about "one out of every seven master trust relationships," notes Jeff Wessel. The bank's share among the Fortune 300 companies is approximately 25 percent.

What exactly is a master trustee? Figure 11–5 shows that the core of the business is basic asset custody—trade settlement, income collection, safekeeping, pricing, and reporting.

In multiple-plan, multiple-manager situations, the bank builds on these basic elements to provide a full range of ancillary services such as global custody, benefit payments, performance measurement and analysis, investment management,

FIGURE 11–5
Master Trust Services

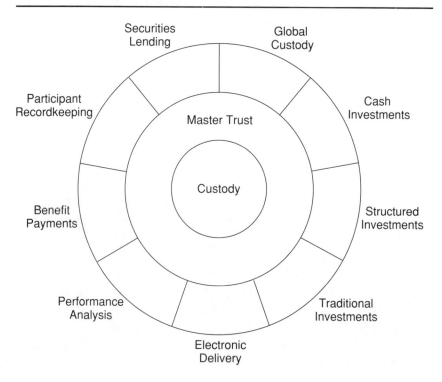

securities lending, and on-line access to accounting investment, and performance information via the bank's electronic delivery system.

These custodial and fiduciary services are provided to three major markets: U.S. corporations, Erisa employee benefit plans, public funds, and taxable asset pools. Corporate Erisa is the largest and oldest segment served. The public funds sector, consisting of retirement funds of states and large municipalities, represents a virtually untapped market of more than $600 billion in over 500 funds. The bank now has 17 clients in this market segment, with more than $18 billion of assets under custody, including the $7.5 billion Colorado State employees fund which recently selected Northern Trust as master custodian for all domestic and global assets.

In the taxable market, which includes foundations, endowments, and other not-for-profit organizations as well as high net worth individuals, the bank has carved out a unique niche by combining personal trust experience and master trust technology. Northern Trust is the Number 1 provider of master custody services for foundations and is rapidly increasing its endowment client base with the recent addition of the University of Chicago and Vanderbilt University. Looking ahead, the bank believes postretirement health care plans may open up yet another market with great potential.

COPING WITH SLOWER GROWTH

Because of the maturity of the master trust market, future growth in assets under management will most likely come from increased market share as industry participants leave the master trust business, according to the bank analysts at Salomon Brothers. To bolster this slowing growth curve, Northern Trust can point to early involvement in two relatively new markets for master services—global custody and public funds management—which should see increasing competition in the next several years.

Through Northern Trust's London office, which was started in 1983 and which had $1 billion in international master trust assets under administration by the end of the year, the firm has fine-tuned the "how-tos" of dealing with extremely variable European clearing systems and has in place a fully trained, experienced staff. (By year-end 1987 the company had $6 billion in international assets under administration.) This presents a clear advantage in the face of the complexities of certain unautomated European markets.

Northern Trust should be able to boost its volume of assets under administration at the expense of start-up competitors, thus significantly enlarging trust fee income. Asset volume will be the key to increased profits, given the similarity in fee structure for both global and domestic custody services. In addition, Northern Trust's five-year experience in this area could mean greater operating efficiency and fewer costly mistakes. Both could offer significant margin protection, especially in the face of what is anticipated to be stronger industry competition.

PUBLIC FUNDS MANAGEMENT

Northern Trust has also been an early entrant into the relatively new public funds management area. In past years strict state regulations governed the outside master trust administration of university, municipal, and other public funds. These have recently been relaxed, thus opening a potential market of $575 billion in assets spread over 400 funds. Within the past two years, the company has developed a customer base with 15 clients and $10 billion in assets under management, while three of its largest competitors in this area (Chase Manhattan, State Street, and Boston Safe Deposit and Trust Company, a subsidiary of the Boston Company that, in turn, is owned by Shearson Lehman) have approximately 18–20 clients each.

As state regulations become more relaxed and foster an increasingly competitive environment for master trustees in the public funds management arena, Northern Trust's longstanding expertise in the administration of master trusts should prove highly transferable to this new market and will constitute an important advantage in expanding the company's customer base.

A SERVICE LESSON

Success in master trust services depends on listening to clients and responding to their special requirements, not simply selling off-the-shelf technology. Northern Trust's experience with the Ford Foundation, the world's largest foundation, is an example of the bank's client-driven approach.

Northern Trust has developed a total information, portfolio management, and general ledger system for Ford that is on-line and interactive. Data on trades are entered into 10 microcomputers in the Foundation's offices and transmitted to Chicago. Early the next day, detailed reports on Ford's many different accounts are available, including information on the latest changes in positions, the confirmation of securities trades, and analyses of holdings based on hundreds of variables. General ledger entries are made automatically.

WORKING TOGETHER

One of the interesting aspects of how Northern Trust operates is its emphasis on teamwork. Chairman Weston Christopherson, a nonbanker who used to head the Jewel Supermarket chain, has emphasized teamwork and the importance of knowing what other parts of the ranks are doing ever since he joined the bank in 1983. And it's paying off.

Thanks to the teamwork of numerous Northern departments, Corporate Financial Services (CFS) recently landed its largest piece of business ever by adding Pacific Telesis Group to its roster of Master Trust clients.

Exceptional support and unusually rapid turnaround from CFS Marketing, Trust Operations, Word Processing, and Graphic Services enabled the bank to capture this $8 billion account, according to Jeff Wessel, executive vice president and head of CFS.

"We could not have achieved this victory without the enthusiastic and unselfish support of many people from other parts of our organization, thus making it a true Northern team effort," said Chairman Christopherson.

PacTel, an offshoot company of AT&T, received notice in late January from their master-trustee, Bank of America, that the bank was exiting the master trust business as of March 31, 1988. Bank of America's decision forced PacTel to face the complicated task of selecting a new trustee in record time.

Northern Trust was one of eight banks selected to receive PacTel's RFP (Request for Proposal) for Master Trust services. The RFP, received on February 2, was due back at PacTel by February 16.

Jim McColl, vice president of CFS Sales, worked with marketing reps Kelly Summerwill, Karen Chessman, and Dave Bieda to put together the initial responses to the largest RFP ever received by Corporate Financial Services.

On February 12, the Word Processing Department was put on red alert. A holiday weekend was approaching, but so was the RFP deadline. Could they help? The word processing staff agreed to work through the long weekend to prepare the copy for the CFS review team.

Jim McColl and Doug Mitchell, senior vice president and head of the Corporate ERISA team, spent Saturday working with Word Processing to clean up the copy. On Sunday the entire CFS SWAT team added their final comments for Word Processing's input on Monday (President's Day).

The perfected RFP was then "Fed-Xed" to John Strahorn, vice president of the Los Angeles office. He flew to San Francisco to hand-deliver the package to PacTel.

The good news came the next week. PacTel had selected the bank as one of the three finalists, along with State Street and Mellon, for this master trust business. But the bad news was that the bank had only six days, counting the weekend, to put together a four-hour presentation of slides, script, and a 100-page booklet that would answer PacTel's specific concerns.

"To showcase the broad range of talents Northern staff has to offer PacTel, we determined that the presentation team should be a departure from our usual sales-oriented one. We put together a specially selected team from several departments that could address all of PacTel's hot buttons," said Mr. Wessel.

The CFS SWAT team, joined by Senior Vice President Tom Kimen, went to work in overtime mode with the designated presentation team: Vice Chairman Bob Reusche; Jim Mitchell, executive vice president and head of Trust Operations; Vice Presidents Deb Maschoff (Administration), Jana Schreuder (Accounting and Transition), Rich Steward (Electronic Delivery System), John Strahorn (Relationship Manager); and Jeff O'Neill, second vice president (Electronic Delivery System). The combined teams formalized the attack plan.

On Thursday, February 25, the SOS went out to Graphic Services. Top quality presentation slides were needed by the following Monday. On Tuesday, March 1, the presentation team made its pitch at PacTel's San Francisco headquarters. Then began the wait.

"We knew we had done a superior job in our presentation," said Bob Reusche. "We stressed the partnership approach we would offer PacTel, the quality of Northern Trust Staff, and our state-of-the-art technology, especially our Number 1 rated on-line Electronic Delivery System. PacTel's vice chairman was so impressed with our presentation that he asked us to remain beyond our allotted time for additional discussion."

The anticipated phone call came early on Tuesday morning, March 8. Teamwork did the job and Northern Trust landed its biggest master trust deal.

A MATTER OF TRUST

Many banks have found the trust business something less than profitable. One of the banks profiled in this book, Point West Bancorp in Sacramento, explored the possibility of offering trust services and decided that it would not be profitable enough.

This is a problem with the trust business. Profits can often be marginal. In addition, it is a business that demands specialists. Not everyone, and not every banker, can walk in and become an effective bank trust officer without experience and know-how.

Yet, it is a business that is growing and offers those banks that can handle it great potential.

One solution, perhaps the only one for the majority of banks, is to align with a bank having a superior trust operations such as the one at Northern Trust. This provides a bank's customers with knowledgeable people who have a fine track record and can add to the bank's bottom line with little expense, and even less risk. Is there anything better in this era of deregulation and competition—and a tightening squeeze on profits?

CHAPTER 12

DEPOSITS ARE ITS MOST IMPORTANT PRODUCT
Republic New York's Approach
to Banking Success.

Before I pray for my
wife and children at
night, I pray for
lower interest rates.
—*Senator Jake Garn*

Most banks are driven by loans. That's where the customers are, they say, over on the left side of the balance sheet; the borrowers are the customers who supply loan assets.

But that's not how Republic National Bank of New York and its holding company, Republic New York Corporation, view the banking business. The management considers that the bank's most important customers are those on the right side of the balance sheet—the depositors.

As Republic president Jeffrey C. Keil puts it, the bank's first duty is to its depositors. "They come to us for security and we allow them to sleep soundly."

This philosophy was borne out after the stock market crash on October 19, 1987. Deposits at Republic rose dramatically in the weeks following the crash as people looked for a safer place for their money.

While this is certainly not a new concept in banking, the emphasis on deposits is relatively rare in the United States. However, it does appear that an increasing number of banks are looking anew at the concept, particularly those institutions which have had serious problems with asset management.

If any bank is contemplating placing an emphasis on deposits and wishes to know how to do it, Republic may be as good an example of the deposit-driven bank that can be found on this side of the Atlantic Ocean.

AMERICAN BANKING, EUROPEAN STYLE

"One thing that makes us unique," says Thomas F. Robards, executive vice president and treasurer, "is that we have a global perspective. People want their wealth managed in such a way as to keep pace with what goes on economically *and* politically."

Republic gets this global perspective naturally. The bank was founded by Lebanese banker Edmond J. Safra in 1966.

Safra, who has a reputation as a somewhat mysterious international banker, brought to his New York operation a private banking style that has been part of his family's tradition for years.

Today, the bank is run by a mostly American management team, but always under the watchful eye and guidance of Mr. Safra.

Earlier this year, Republic opened a subsidiary in Geneva, Switzerland. Named the Republic National Bank of New York (Suisse), the new unit actually replaces the Trade and Development Bank, which was Safra's first bank and which he sold to American Express in 1983.

As part of the sale, Safra continued to run the bank for a couple of years for the new owners. But his management style, as well as his emphasis on deposits, did not mesh too well with American Express. He left the Swiss bank in 1985; in the separation agreement, the Lebanese banker was barred from operating a bank in Switzerland for three years. That period of time concluded on February 29, 1988. The new subsidary opened for business the following day, on March 1.

Edmond Safra is chairman of the Swiss subsidiary, as well as honorary chairman of Republic New York Corporation. Shortly after the new bank opened, Michael Cartillier, general manager of the subsidiary, voiced Safra's mode of operation when he stated, "In Switzerland, as in all Republic banks, the highest priority will be the protection of depositors' assets."

It is expected that the Geneva bank will attract a sizeable number of depositors from the old Trade and Development Bank. In fact, analysts consider the new banking subsidiary such a solid investment, they predict it will add as much as $2.50 per share to Republic's earnings by 1990. And in 1988, investment analysts such as Keefe Bruyette expect Republic to earn approximately $5.65 a share.

Obviously, the deposit route to profits seems to be working at Republic New York Corporation.

LIABILITY AND ASSET MANAGEMENT AT REPUBLIC

In general Republic's assets are selected to match approximately both the maturity and interest sensitivity of the liabilities. Thus, the composition of the bank's liabilities determines the composition of its assets.

This management policy has two important implications. First, liquidity requirements are met because assets generally mature when liabilities mature. Second, changes in the levels of interest rates do not affect the bank significantly since both assets and liabilities have approximately the same sensitivity to interest rate changes.

Diversification is another principle employed in the management of liabilities and assets at Republic. The corporation is active in international banking and, in managing this activity, diversifies risk among many regions and countries throughout the world. Liabilities, which are mostly interest-bearing deposits, are obtained from both domestic and international sources. These sources of funds represent a wide range of depositors, mostly individuals, and various types of deposits. The diversification of the bank's funding sources provides stability in attracting funds. In managing its asset structure, creditworthiness of customers is an important factor.

Republic's primary funding source is deposits which are

principally interest bearing. Deposits in foreign offices have accounted for more than half of these funds in each of the last three years. Through its domestic branch network, the bank obtains a diverse base of retail time and savings deposits in both the short-term and long-term markets. The increase in domestic office interest-bearing deposits is primarily attributable to the addition of the Williamsburgh Savings Bank which has a Network of thirteen branches. Republic's program of issuing Certificate of Deposit Notes ("Deposit Notes") which are long-term deposits sold to institutional and corporate investors has increased substantially since 1986 when the program was started.

FOREIGN DEPOSITS

The banks' deposits from foreign sources in both domestic and foreign branch offices and foreign banking subsidiaries have contributed substantially to Republic's deposit growth. Average deposits in foreign offices were $7.5 billion in 1987, $6.8 billion in 1986, and $5.4 billion in 1985, representing more than 50 percent of the total average deposits in each of the last three years. The company continues to place increased emphasis on overseas banking operations, particularly in the International Private Banking Group which has generated a substantial portion of these deposits.

GROWTH THROUGH DEPOSITS

Most banks' earnings are driven by loan demand, and they then purchase money to "fund" the loans. Thus, earnings growth depends on loan demand. At Republic earnings are driven by the deposit base. As most depositors leave their funds in the bank, the deposit base has built-in natural growth as interest is earned. Thus, Republic's growth should be less cyclical than virtually any other bank's.

In keeping with its depositor focus the company's acquisition policy has been aimed at buying deposits. The only major acquisition to date has been that of the Williamsburgh Savings Bank, an institution that had an interest rate mismatch problem but not credit problems. The cost to Republic was a cash payment of $10 million to the depositors, $5 million for an early retirement program, and the assumption of $45 million in goodwill. In addition, Republic downstreamed $200 million in capital, but retained the funds on its consolidated balance sheet. For all this (a total cash cost of about $15 million) the company picked up $2.2 billion in deposits. The unit is currently earning about $3 million per month.

THE FLOW OF FUNDS

Although the financial statements issued by Republic delineate foreign and domestic depositors (See Table 12–1), funds flows are really far more sophisticated.

The bank looks for opportunities of the moment so that, for instance, domestic depositors' funds may be transferred overseas to take advantage of superior investment opportunities. The bank looks first at the profitability and cost, not necessarily growth, in any one area.

Over the last 10 years the bank has grown its total deposit balances at a 22 percent compound growth rate. Domestic deposits have grown at 11 percent and foreign deposits at 37 percent whereas, in 1977, 78 percent of the bank's deposits were domestic, at the end of 1986 that figure had fallen to 35 percent.

Over the last five years Republic has expanded its franchise, especially in the overseas market. Foreign deposits have grown at a 25 percent compound rate, four times the growth in the domestic area.

The great majority of deposit growth has come in the form of time deposits of individuals, partnerships, and corporations, with a more modest increase in deposits of governments and official institutions. Foreign deposits by banks have declined. In aggregate though, foreign deposits increased from 45 percent of the total in 1981 to 65 percent in 1986. When foreign deposits in domestic offices are included, the percentages are 69 percent and 82 percent respectively.

TABLE 12–1
Republic's Deposits ($ thousands)

	1987	1986	1985
Domestic Offices:			
Non-interest bearing deposits:			
Individuals, partnerships and corporations	$ 599,288	$ 561,083	$ 410,402
Foreign governments and official institutions	2.629	1,055	1,295
U.S. Government and states and political subdivisions	3,647	3,824	3,879
Banks	33,440	29,029	20,173
Certified and official checks	57,525	60,624	39,717
Total non-interest bearing deposits	696,529	655,615	475,466
Interest bearing deposits:			
Savings and NOW accounts	844,262	216,130	140,914
Money market accounts	1,151,657	919,653	740,391
Deposit notes	650,000	450,000	—
Individuals, partnerships and corporations	3,910,264	1,938,909	1,822,077
U.S. Government and states and political subdivisions	54,813	19,705	39,575
Banks	32,611	36,725	—
Total interest bearing deposits	6,643,607	3,581,122	2,742,957
Total deposits in domestic offices	7,340,136	4,236,737	3,218,423
Foreign offices:			
Non-interest bearing deposits in foreign offices	125,379	104,748	54,194
Interest bearing deposits in foreign offices	7,373,031	6,455,882	6,456,604
Total deposits in foreign offices	7,498,410	6,560,630	6,510,798
Total deposits	$14,838,546	$10,797,367	$9,729,221

DEPOSITOR PROFILE

The company gathers deposits from three sources: individuals in the New York City area, foreign individuals, and professional money managers. Each of these sources comprises about one-third of the total deposit base.

Within New York, Republic targets the "investor-saver," or a depositor who is typically 45–65 years old with an average balance of $40,000–$50,000, or about four times his or her NYC peers. These deposits are gathered through Republic's 29 branches and Williamsburgh's 13 branches in New York City.

Another third of the deposits is gathered from wealthy individuals in 80 countries around the world. The typical depositor is an entrepreneur or merchant who, having taken business risk within his country, is seeking to protect part of his capital from political or economical risk. The average account size is $400,000–$500,000. This is the type of depositor who will be attracted to the new Swiss bank.

The final third of deposits comes from professional money managers. Republic takes this money only to gain a very small spread by investing the funds on a short-term basis in interbank deposits with an average maturity of less than three months. Entailing little risk, this arbitrage of funds adds to the bottom line, but also tends to bloat the balance sheet and reduce the return on assets.

There are two important points to be made about the bank's deposit base. First, Republic's foreign deposits are largely from individuals, not "hot" money as is often the case in other banks with sizeable foreign deposits. Second, Republic's depositors make very few transactions. This means less overhead for the bank. It also means that most depositors allow their interest to accrue. As a result, Republic is able to lock in deposit growth in the 5–7 percent range on an annual basis.

DIFFERENT LENDING, TOO

Republic generally does not like the risk profile of traditional bank lending and so has kept an underweighted portfolio of loans in relation to assets.

Its loan portfolio is remarkably short-lived, with over 64 percent of the balances (other than residential mortgages) having a scheduled maturity of less than one year. The residential mortgages, which comprise 32 percent of the total portfolio, have a weighted average loan-to-value ratio of 55 percent, a figure that is 25 percent below industry standards.

In addition, there are no agricultural, shipping, oil and gas, construction, nor leveraged buy-out loans on the books.

The only significant failure has been in its assumption that lending to governments was low risk, a mistake committed by a great many legendary bankers.

Since 1983, Republic has reduced its net sovereign debt exposure by an estimated 60 percent to $300 million through write-offs, marking portions of the portfolio to market, and through asset sales. Its exposure, in order of importance, is to Mexico, Brazil, Argentina, Venezuela, and Chile. Republic added $100 million to its reserves for foreign debt in the second quarter of 1987.

The bank's exposure as a percent of equity is in the neighborhood of 25 percent versus an average at the eight major money center banks of 125 percent. Were Republic to write off totally its unreserved portion of sovereign debt, it would still have a higher equity-to-asset ratio than any other major New York bank except J. P. Morgan.

A WORD ABOUT THOSE LDC LOANS

In some ways, Republic's LDC loans are not so much a failure but a lesson in pragmatic management.

During the 1970s lending to lesser developed countries was a highly profitable business for many banks. Even if it had been possible to forecast the problems that eventually arose, few bank managements would have had the support of their boards to have turned away from loans that seemed lucrative and low risk.

When Mexico defaulted on its interest payments and the quality of LDC loans was first called into question in 1982, many industry spokesmen (including Citicorp's Walter Wriston) reassured themselves that "countries don't go bankrupt" and denied the existence of a long-term problem. But not Republic. It quietly began to shore up its capital base through retained earnings, preferred and common stock offerings, writedowns of loans, and additions to the loan-loss reserve to the detriment of current earnings.

In other words, John Reed at Citicorp got considerable praise for recognizing the true value of his bank's LDC protfolio in the spring of 1987 and set aside reserves against the loans. Republic began this process four years earlier.

OTHER PROFIT CENTERS

Republic has a number of other areas of income generation.

• Commissions from the issuance of letters of credit. The bank's outstanding standby LOCs, guarantees and other LOCs stood at $1,080 million at year-end 1986. This level of off-balance sheet commitment is much lower than the bank's peers, and the underwriting criteria are very strenuous.
• Commissions from acceptances (i.e., short-term secured obligations that finance international trade).
• Commissions from the bank note business. This area deals primarily with the physical transfer of currencies for clients. This is a volume-driven business with a cost structure and network that presents serious barriers to entry.
• Trading and investment securities gains. This business depends upon selling at a higher price than the cost paid and works better in a declining rate environment than a rising rate environment. In addition, Republic has taken securities gains to offset the write down of certain Latin American outstandings.
• Foreign exchange—foreign currency bank note trading. This is mostly a volume-driven business which has been profitable in each of the last 10 years.
• Precious metals—the bank carries a precious metal inventory (gold and silver) which the bank hedges 90–95 percent. In addition to trading metals, the bank also buys and sells options and sells the metals to individuals and commercial end users. This business has been consistently profitable over the last ten years.

Republic has recently been receiving the (belated) attention of a number of bank stock analysts. Marshwinds Advisory Company in Georgia provided an interesting profile of the bank as it related to investors:

Features	Benefits
1. Edmond Safra owns 1/3 of the common stock.	1. Management's interest same as client's.
2. Basic principle is the safe-guarding of depositors' funds.	2. Safe depositors' funds lead to safe shareholders' funds.
3. Dividend has increased each year for 10 years.	3. Client gets higher cash return over time.
4. The Board has a stated policy of paying 25% to 30% of net earnings as dividends.	4. Improved earnings will flow through as higher dividends.
5. Expansion to global bank is almost complete.	5. Higher profits from receding start-up costs.
6. LDC loans are less than 3% of assets.	6. LDC loans are manageable.
7. Management policy is to match assets and liabilities.	7. Higher interest rates will have little effect on bank.
8. Deposit growth should accelerate in 1988.	8. More assets and stable ROA equals higher profits.

This private bank, it could be said, it its own best example of how a deposit-driven bank should be run. It seems safe to state that international banker Edmond Safra, who owns close to 40 percent of Republic, is rather pleased with the management performance of his bank.

DEPOSITS CAN BUILD PROFITS

Not every bank can be run like Republic National Bank of New York. It is essentially a private bank and *only* a private bank.

Tom Robards observed that many people going into the business of private banking look at the concept as "another market we can lend to." That is not how Republic looks at its business. As Robards says, "We are not interested in financing consumption."

But other banks can look at private banking as another service to be performed for a specific group of customers. In the past few years a number of banks have been doing just that with varying degrees of success.

One of the keys to private banking profitability is to have staff people who can deal with people of wealth and can properly service their needs. This requires different skills than those needed for commercial lending or consumer finance. With more and more bankers going into private banking, qualified private bankers are becoming a scarce commodity.

Of course, true private banking requires a particular approach for dealing with the balance sheet as the Republic story explains. For most banks, where private banking is just another specialized service, this is impossible. But it should be realized that, because of this, the full potential of the private banking business will not be completely realized.

Driven by Deposits. It is possible, of course, for a bank to drive itself to bring in more deposits.

Building deposits can be relatively easy for a bank to do— if it is willing to pay enough for them, particularly through the use of generous rates on certificates of deposit and money market accounts. But the high costs of funds lowers the value of such deposits to a bank. The trick is to pay to going rate, or slightly above, and then provide the services necessary to keep those funds with the bank.

A bank must try to bring in deposits via interest-free accounts, NOW accounts, and pass book savings. Yet this may not be enough.

There are other things a bank can do. For example, it should not shy away from going after customers of other banks. If a customer at a competitive financial institution has, say, significant idle balances at his present bank, he could be informed about how your bank can make his money do more for him. Cash management accounts and money market investments are natural vehicles to attract such customers.

Corporate deposits, of course, can boost a bank's deposit base quite rapidly. Many companies can be attracted to CDs and money market accounts, if approached properly. Point West Bank in California (see Chapter 10) has had considerable success with a money market account that was specifically tailored to the needs of business firms.

At this point in time, unfortunately, there is an awful lot of competition out there for the deposit business. Still, the safety of funds in banks, and the relative liquidity banks provide, are strong selling points. And those selling points should be used.

PART 5

DEMANDS OF A CHANGING BANKING ENVIRONMENT

Today—and tomorrow, of course—may be the most exciting time the banking industry has ever known. Exciting in the sense of new developments, great challenges, and nearly limitless opportunities for bank organizations and banking professionals.

For someone entering banking now, following graduation from college, the career potential is tremendous, and difficult to match in any other type of business. For someone trying to decide what route to take for a working life, why not opt for an industry where there is good pay, interesting work, a growing receptiveness to innovation and creative ideas, travel, terrific learning possibilities, and the promise of an even brighter future?

With only slight exaggeration, this is what banking—or perhaps more accurately, the financial services industry—has become. At least, this is the case at those financial institutions which are making the most of what deregulation and the competitive forces presently at work have brought about.

All this is a far cry from what banking used to be. The banking environment has changed and continues to change. Among other things, and at the very least, it means that bank management must cope with change, must manage the change—and move beyond the changes taking place.

Without question, heavy demands are being placed upon management by the changing banking environment. Some of these demands have been alluded to, if not explored, in this book. Others have been noted only in passing. Yet all need to be addressed by banking companies if they expect to be around during the next decade.

HARNESSING TECHNOLOGY

This is the one demand of the banking environment where there truly are no boundaries, or at least where they are not yet known. It is an area so dynamic, so complex, that a bank is well-advised to maintain an open mind and be flexible enough to take advantage of new developments as they arise.

This is the stance taken by most banks that are doing reasonably well in using technology—First Wisconsin, of course, but also such banks as First Wachovia, Security Pacific, and BancOne, to name a few.

The larger banks, with widespread locations and diverse product lines, must use technology or they won't be able to deal with the challenges of size. Yet smaller banks, including the smallest, cannot ignore electronic banking if they expect to serve their customers adequately.

There are two major problems associated with banking technology—personnel and costs. The cost of technology is high and the demand for trained people is even higher. Fortunately, small banks are able to turn to outside suppliers, including larger banks, to satisfy their processing and information needs. However, the twin problems of personnel and costs are likely to plague banking for some time to come.

CONTENDING WITH COMPETITION

For a great many banks during most of the years of their existence, competition was something other types of businesses had to worry about. That has never been true for some banks in some markets, but, for most, competition was little more than a word.

But all this changed forever with deregulation and the entry of nonbanking companies into the financial marketplace.

Now a financial institution must contend both with other financial institutions—banks with banks, thrifts with thrifts, banks with thrifts—and with companies such as American Express, Merrill Lynch, Prudential, finance companies, leasing companies, and a list of other companies that continues to grow.

The range and the depth of the competition today means that a bank must be ready for assault from all sides in a given market. It must be ready, not only with service and products, but with promotional campaigns that target the chosen customer and with advertising that makes the customer sit up and take (favorable) notice.

Glenfed, as discussed earlier, is a good example of a financial organization that is doing what it can to meet the competition in its two major markets, California and Florida. It also is an example of an institution that has redefined its market by narrowing the scope of its product line in order to concentrate on products within its specific field of expertise—real estate.

Contending with the competition, then, is a demand that requires a bank to be the best it can be—and to accept what it cannot be.

SOPHISTICATED, SAVVY CUSTOMERS

If it can be said that banking isn't what it used to be, the same statement can be made about bank customers.

This is a time when lender liability suits are being filed with increasing regularity, accusing banks of improper lending practices and more improper collection activities. Just as importantly, the borrowers are winning many of the suits.

Individuals are much more concerned—as well as more knowledgeable—about financial matters. They want the best return possible on their money; they are also becoming adept at moving funds from one account to another and from one institution to another. They want their resources profitably managed.

This has come about, in part, because of the education being given them by financial institutions through new and/or expanded services in these areas, and the education they are receiving through advertising and through money management programs available via books and television.

Companies are also more concerned about the effective management of corporate funds. They have discovered that they are able to use other methods to raise funds; no longer are bank loans the only way to go. As a result, they have discovered they don't have to rely as heavily on banks any more, and they aren't.

This financial sophistication on the part of customers, corporate and individual, large and small, has meant that banks must scramble for those customers. Even when they can provide the desired products, they must also provide the best possible service. It has also meant that adding new customers is a more complex and difficult proposition.

One thing you can bank upon—customers for financial services and products are not going to be any less sophisticated or less knowledgeable about financial matters in the 1990s.

EXPAND OR DIE

Growth is the watchword for banking in the late 1980s. For banks of size, this often (but not always) means taking advantage of the reciprocal banking laws allowing expansion into neighboring or other states.

It was those banking laws that helped bring together Sun Banks and the Trust Company of Georgia and the Third National Corporation of Nashville. But it has not been laws which have made the combine work. The new organization is moving smartly ahead because of the efforts of Robert Strickland, Joel Wells, and countless others in those southeastern banking companies.

The driving force propelling Carl Reichardt and Wells

Fargo Bank forward has been growth, including the desire to expand market share. It is also the realization on the part of an increasing number of bankers such as Mr. Reichardt that not growing means losing ground to others.

Yet managing growth is not easy. Some—again, Continental Illinois comes to mind—have not properly managed growth and so have suffered the consequences. This is surely one of the great demands of our changing banking environment. And one of the most difficult to meet.

THE HUMAN FACTOR

Encompassing all the other demands, and so creating its own, is the human factor in banking.

Finding sufficient numbers of able, trained people is a problem many, if not all, banks face today. Without question, this will be an ongoing problem as the banking environment continues to change.

One complication, however, is that the skills required by modern banking companies are also changing. Already mentioned is the need for people to manage and operate the new technology. In addition, there is the increasing emphasis being placed on marketing and sales skills.

In-house training programs will help, but only for the banks large enough to conduct them. It is to be hoped that as the word about the "new" banking gets around, high-caliber college graduates will be attracted to the industry which, as was pointed out at the beginning of this chapter, has become an exciting place to be.

At the same time, there is a concern that the colleges, and the high schools as well, are not always providing the courses that will help prepare young people for employment in banking—or in other businesses, either. Perhaps what is required is input and joint efforts in educational programs at both the secondary and college levels. This would be an opportunity to lead the way with cooperative programs that could assist youth to meet the challenges of working careers.

MORE SUPER BANKS

A dozen banks performing superbly in certain specific areas have been profiled in this book. There are others, of course, that could be included in the category of "super banking" performers.

At the same time, the demands being placed on financial institutions in this changing banking environment make one thing quite clear—the industry will need more super banks in the years ahead.

INDEX

V

Variable rate mortgages, 147
Virginia Commonwealth Bankshares.
    See Signet Banking Corporation

W

Wells, Joel R., 18, 20–22, 198
Wells Fargo, 36–49
    acquisition, benefits of, 44, 46
    automated teller systems,
        integration of, 43–44
    Barclays Bank of California,
        acquisition of, 47
    consolidation, 38, 42, 43
    core business areas, 37
    cost control, 38, 46

Wells Fargo—(*continued*)
    credit card operations, 42, 44, 47
    Crocker National Corporation,
        acquisition of, 36, 38–45
    customer retention, 42, 48
    deregulation strategy, 37
    employee bonuses, 45
    financial performance, 39, 45,
        47
    foreign loans, 38, 44
    Fox Pitt, Kelton, Inc., evaluation
        by, 46
    investment services, 37
    management style, 37
    Paine Webber, evaluation by, 46
    personnel, attrition of, 42–43, 49
    Shearson Lehman Hutton,
        evaluation by, 46–47